Famous Murders, Riots, Disasters, and Crooked Politicians - New York City - 1834 to 1938

By - JOE BRUNO

Editor - LAWRENCE VENTURATO

Published by - KNICKERBOCKER PUBLISHING COMPANY

Part 1 - Murders:

The Murder of Helen Jewett by Richard Robinson - 1837

She was a beautiful prostitute; he was a handsome clerk. They seemed destined to live together, happily ever after. Yet, when the disfigured and charred body of 23-year-old Helen Jewett was found smoldering on April, 10, 1836, in a brothel bed at 41 Thomas Street in downtown Manhattan, the prime and only suspect in her murder was her boyfriend, 19-year-old Richard Robinson.

Helen Jewett was born Doras Doyen in Augusta, Maine in 1813. Her father died when she was 13, but a local judge, smitten by her remarkable beauty, took her under his wing. This judge spent a small fortune on Doras' education, and he provided her with all the tools she needed to attain a successful status in life.

Like a wild stallion needing to run free, Doras, at the age of 17, abandoned her benefactor and took off with a prosperous young banker from Portland, Maine. In Portland, the banker provided Doras with every luxury. They lived in a palatial mansion, where swanky parties and flowing champagne were the order of the day and especially of the night.

It was apparently during this period of time that Doras first became a prostitute. Yet, Doras was an impetuous person. She and the banker quarreled often, and finally, Doras left him flat. She traveled to New York City, and she changed her name to Helen Jewett.

In New York City, Helen Jewett threw herself eagerly into the profession of prostitution; working in the most luxurious brothels in town. To increase her business, Helen used to stroll invitingly down Broadway searching for old flames or for new men to seduce. Helen always dressed entirely in shades of green, which matched the color of her captivating eyes. As a result, Helen became known as "The Girl in Green." In time, Helen was the most sought-after prostitute in New York City. It was said Helen had a voracious sexual appetite, and she enjoyed the company of several wealthy men each night, sometimes in groups or two or more.

Helen's beauty was such, Warden Charles Sutton wrote in his book, *The History of the New York Tombs,* "She was beautifully formed; had large green eyes which snapped with mischievousness and one of the most fascinating faces that ever imperiled a susceptible observer. Her disposition was as beautiful as her face and figure, and she was charitable to a fault with all who required assistance."

Richard Robinson was born in Durham, Connecticut in 1818. His parents had considerable means, and they spared no expense in raising and educating their young boy. Richard grew up to be a very handsome young man, tall and broad, and always immaculately dressed. Yet Richard, like Helen, was a free spirit, and when he reached the age of 17, he ran away from his parents' home and absconded to New York City.

Richard, due to the fine education he had received through the good grace of his parents, was immediately hired at a dry goods store on Maiden Lane owned by Joseph Hoxie. Richard soon became what the people of those times called a "roisterer," or someone who was part of the "jet set," motoring about from one fine event to another with nary a care in the world. Richard made a fine appearance, resplendent with dark curly hair and dressed in his usual rich Spanish cloak.

As fate would have it, Richard was entering a downtown theater when he saw a thug attack a beautiful young woman, who was also about to enter the same theater. Richard, by far the bigger man, was able to easily throttle the ruffian, thereby thrusting himself as a hero in the young woman's eyes. This young woman was none other than Helen Jewett.

Immediately enthralled with the handsome young man, Helen handed Robinson a business card that read, "Helen Jewett, Palais de la Duchesse Berri." This was Helen way of telling Robinson that she was a high-class prostitute, who only serviced the upper crust of society.

The place where Helen worked at that time was what was called, "a furnished resort," owned by Mme. Berri on Duane Street. Soon, Robinson became a frequent visitor of Helen at Mme. Berri's. Instead of using his real name, Robinson introduced himself to Mme. Berri as "Frank Rivers." This was a common practice at the time, since men who had respectable jobs didn't want people working in not–so–respectable places, like brothels, to know their real names.

Within a few weeks, Helen, although she was four years older than Robinson, was obviously more infatuated with Robinson than he was with her. Sensing something was wrong, Helen was obsessed by the idea that Robinson was possibly sharing his affections with another woman. One night, Helen disguised herself as a boy, and she followed Robinson around Lower Manhattan. After he had made the rounds of several bars, Helen spotted Robinson entering a brothel on Broome Street. Helen somehow gained admission to the brothel, and she found Robinson in bed in the embrace of another woman. Incensed, Helen attacked the woman, striking her repeatedly, with blow after blow on the woman's face. Helen's gaudy diamond rings slashed several bloody tears in the woman's cheeks, forehead, and nose.

Robinson was incredulous at the ferocity of Helen's attacks, and he told her, in no uncertain terms, their relationship was over. Helen was crushed, and she started bombarding Robinson with letter after letter, begging him for forgiveness. But it was not to be. Robinson discarded Helen like an old newspaper, and Helen, dismayed at the turn of events, left New York City for places unknown.

Helen returned to New York City in October 1835, and she immediately became employed at the brothel of Rosina Townsend, located at 41 Thomas Street. As luck would have it, while Helen was strolling on the docks by the East River, she ran into Robinson. They reconciled, and "Frank Rivers" became a frequent visitor at 41 Thomas Street.

A few months later, Helen found out, that while she was away, Robinson had become involved with another girl, who inexplicably had died from ingesting poison, allegedly administered to her by Robinson. Helen confronted Robinson with this accusation, which he vehemently denied. Ultimately, Robinson was able to convince Helen of his innocence in the death of the girl in question. Robinson also told Helen that he was so in love with her, he wanted her to abandon her wicked life at 41 Thomas Street and marry him instead.

On April 10, 1836, Robinson, the cad that he was, informed Helen that not only was he not going to marry her, but that he was, in fact, engaged to be married to a young woman of great wealth and position. Helen was heartbroken.

She wrote Robinson a letter saying, "You know how I have loved, but for God's sake don't compel me to show how I can hate."

On the following day, Robinson wrote Helen a letter in a disguised hand, telling her that he would come to her place of business at 9 p.m. that evening. Robinson also insisted that Helen should be the one to greet him at the front door.

On April 11, 1836, at exactly 9 p.m., "Frank Rivers" knocked at the front door of 41 Thomas Street. However, by coincidence, Rosina Townsend was near the front door at the exact moment Robinson knocked, and she admitted Robinson instead of Helen. As was his custom, Robinson wore his distinctive long Spanish cloak.

Helen, upon hearing Robinson's voice, rushed to the front door and hugged Robinson. She said, "Oh, my dear Frank, how glad I am that you have come."

Robinson and Helen then retired to Helen's apartment.

Marie Stevens was another prostitute, who occupied the apartment next door to Helen's. At approximately 1 a.m., Stevens heard noises emanating from Helen's apartment. Stevens later said it sounded like someone had been struck by a heavy blow, and then the injured person had emitted a long, mournful moan. Moments later, Stevens heard Helen's door being opened. Stevens opened her door just a crack, and she spotted a tall man, wearing a long cloak and holding a dimly lit candle, slither out of Helen's apartment. Terrified, Stevens locked herself in her apartment.

A few minutes later, Stevens heard a knock on the front door. Rosina Townsend answered the front door and admitted another male guest. After this guest went to the apartment of the lady he was visiting, Townsend noticed that there was a lit lamp in the parlor. Townsend examined the lamp and determined it belonged either to Helen, or Stevens. Townsend also noticed that the back door to the building was ajar. She yelled out, "Who's there?" But there was no answer.

Townsend first knocked on Stevens's door. After determining that the lamp did not belong to Stevens, Townsend knocked on Helen's door. Upon hearing no answer, Townsend opened the door to Helen's apartment, and she was overcome by a large cloud of smoke. Townsend's screams aroused the rest of the house's occupants. In a panic, the male guests put on their trousers, dressed quickly and ran from the building, lest they be caught in an embarrassing situation by the authorities.

Townsend opened the window, and she began screaming into the night air, "Fire!"

A night watchman, who was the precursor to the New York City policeman, heard Townsend's cries. He rushed into the house, into Helen's room, and he extinguished the fire. What he saw next, caused Ms. Townsend and the rest of the female inhabitants of the building to scream in horror.

The scantily clad body of Helen Jewett was lying on the bed. Her skull had been split open with three powerful blows, apparently made by a hatchet. Any one of the three blows would have been enough to kill her. The left side of Helen's upper body was charred, from her having been set on fire after she was savagely attacked.

When the authorities searched the backyard at 41 Thomas Street, they found a bloody hatchet, which apparently was the murder weapon. Found next to the hatchet was the type of cloak which Robinson normally wore. Apparently, the murderer had fled out the back door, dropped the hatchet and cloak, and scaled a white fence that had recently been painted. The murderer then fled down a side street, where he was spotted by a Negro woman. The woman said she could not detail the man's facial features, but that his general appearance was similar to that of Robinson.

No one at 41 Thomas Street knew Frank Rivers's real name. However, one of the working girls did know that Frank Rivers worked as a clerk for a merchant in a dry goods shop on Maiden Lane. This young lady also knew the address of that dry goods store.

That night, watchmen Dennis Brink and George Noble went to the dry goods store on Maiden Lane and asked if anyone knew a Frank Rivers. They were told the man they were looking for was actually Richard Robinson, aged 19, and that he lived at a boarding house at 42 Dey Street.

Brink and Noble went to that address and found Robinson in bed. Robinson claimed he had been in his room for many hours. Robinson's roommate verified the fact that Robinson had been home almost the entire night.

Brink and Noble searched the room, and they found Robinson's trousers stained with white paint; the same type of white paint that was on the fence at 41 Thomas Street. As a result, Robinson, although he said he was innocent of all charges, was arrested and taken to the jail on Chambers Street. After an indictment came down, saying there was sufficient evidence to try Robinson for murder, he was taken to a prison cell in Bellevue Hospital on 29th Street, where he was housed with the criminally insane.

Since Robinson came from a wealthy family, his relatives immediately hired the best criminal attorneys in town. These attorneys were up against New York City prosecutors who claimed that Robinson had killed Helen Jewett, because she had threatened to reveal to his present fiancé that he had, in fact, killed his former girlfriend.

The trial was scheduled for June 2, 1836.

Several mysterious circumstances suddenly started working in Robinson's favor. The colored woman, who had seen Helen Jewett's killer run from the scene, mysteriously disappeared. And Marie Stevens, who had seen the killer slip out of Helen Jewett's room, died in her bed before the trial started. It could not be determined if Stevens had died of natural causes, committed suicide, or was murdered.

Without advance notice to the prosecutors, Robinson's lawyers called a man named Robert Furlong to the witness stand. Furlong stated that Robinson, at the time of Helen Jewett's murder, had been, in fact, sitting in Furlong's cigar store, smoking a cigar and reading the newspapers.

Notwithstanding the two missing witnesses and the surprise alibi supplied by Furlong, the case against Robinson seemed to be overwhelming. Robinson was seen entering Helen Jewett's room by Ms. Townsend. In addition, Ms. Townsend said that at 11 p.m. on the night of the murder, she had entered Helen Jewett's room to deliver a bottle of champagne. When she entered the room, she saw both Helen Jewett and Robinson lying on the bed.

The hatchet, which was the murder weapon, was identified by an employee at the dry goods store where Robinson worked as the hatchet that Robinson had used frequently at work. Also, Robinson's roommate admitted on the witness stand, under oath, that Robinson, in fact, had not been home the entire night of Helen Jewett's murder.

After Robinson's lead attorney gave his closing statement, and the district attorney gave his closing statement, the judge inexplicably told the jury that any testimony given by prostitutes, including Ms. Townsend, because of the nature of their employment, should not be believed. This slanted the case decidedly in Robinson's favor. The jury took less than a half an hour to render a verdict of not guilty.

The consensus in the New York City newspapers was that a guilty man had been set free. Two weeks after the trial, Robert Furlong, who had conveniently provided Robinson with an alibi for the time of Helen Jewett's murder, inexplicably killed himself by jumping into the Hudson River. And besides the judge in the case obviously favoring the defendant, it was suspected that several members of the jury had been bought off by Robinson's rich relatives.

However, nothing could be proven and Robinson walked away a free man. The murderer of Helen Jewett was never found, nor can it be ascertained if anyone did, in fact, look for that murderer.

Yet, justice may have been served in an unexpected manner.

Ostracized by the Helen Jewett murder trial, Robinson left New York City and took up residence in the Republic of Texas. Two years later, Robinson contracted an unspecified illness. In a state of delirium, Robinson was taken to a local hospital. Before he died at the age of 21, on his death bed Robinson muttered his last words: "Helen Jewett."

The story of Helen Jewett and Richard Robinson did not end after their deaths. In the following years, their wax figurines traveled in sideshows throughout the northeastern states. The implied message in these traveling shows was that young people should think twice before getting involved in a life that is steeped in decadence and immorality.

The Murder of Mary Rogers – "The Beautiful Cigar Girl" by Daniel Payne -1841

She was known as "The Beautiful Cigar Girl," but the 1841 murder of 20-year-old Mary Rogers remains one of the most baffling unsolved murders in New York City's history.

Rogers was a clerk in the upscale John Anderson's Tobacco Shop in downtown Manhattan. She was an amazingly beautiful girl, and famous writers like Edgar Allen Poe, James Fennimore Cooper, and Washington Irving, became her regular customers. Poet Fitz Green-Halleck was so smitten by Rogers, he wrote a poem in Rogers's honor. Many of the top newspaper editors and beat writers were also frequent customers at Anderson's; some just to get a brief glimpse of Rogers's beauty.

On Sunday morning, July 25, 1841, at a Nassau Street boarding house owned by her mother, Rogers told one of the boarders, her fiancé Daniel Payne, that she was going out for the afternoon to visit her sister, a Mrs. Downing. That night, New York was hit by a severe thunderstorm, and Rogers did not return to the boarding house. Both her mother and Payne figured that because of the storm, Rogers was spending the night at her sister's house.

Yet on the next day, Rogers's sister told them that Rogers had never shown up at all, nor had she expected Rogers to visit. Joined by Rogers's ex-fiancé, Alfred Crommelin, they searched the city, but could find no trace of Rogers.

Unfortunately, this was not the first time that Rogers had disappeared. In October 1838, Rogers's whereabouts were unknown for several days. When she returned, she said she had visited a friend in Brooklyn, even though she had not told her mother, or her employers, of her intentions to do so.

After Rogers's second disappearance, Rogers's mother placed an ad in the *New York Sun* daily newspaper, asking if anyone knew "the whereabouts of a young lady, aged 20, last seen on the morning of the 25th, who was wearing a white dress, black shawl, blue scarf, Leghorn hat, light colored shoes, and light-colored parasol."

No one responded to the ad.

On Wednesday, July 28, at Sybil's Cave in Hoboken, New

Jersey, three men spotted something floating and bobbing on the New Jersey side of the Hudson River. The men jumped in a rowboat, and they quickly rowed to the area where the object was located. When they got there, they found the dead body of a young woman. They tired pulling the body onto the rowboat, but after a few unsuccessful attempts, they tied a rope under the dead woman's chin and rowed toward shore.

When the coroner examined the body, in addition to severe discoloration all over her once- beautiful face, he found a red mark, the shape of a man's thumb, on the right side of her neck. There were also several marks on the left side of her neck, the size of a man's finger, indicating Rogers had been strangled and her body dumped in the river. Crommelin, after reading the accounts in the newspapers of the body found in the Hudson River, traveled to Hoboken, and he identified the body as that of Mary Rogers.

Because of her popularity with the press, Rogers's death became front-page news in all the New York City newspapers. Members of the press cast suspicion on her fiancé Daniel Payne, who had told the police, that on the day of Rogers' disappearance, he had visited his brother and had spent the day bouncing to and from several bars and restaurants in New York City. To prove his innocence, Payne produced sworn affidavits from witnesses, saying he was indeed where he said he was on the day Rogers had disappeared.

The mystery of Rogers's death soon disappeared from the daily newspapers. The New York City police then consisted of motley night-time Watchmen and day-time Roundsmen, who were untrained and lowly paid commoners, with little incentive to solve crimes. These pseudo-policemen decided not to investigate any further, since the body of Rogers was found in New Jersey. The New Jersey police felt Rogers had most likely been killed in New York City and that the murder investigation was not their problem.

Frederica Loss owned a tavern called Nick Moore's House, near Hoboken, New Jersey, not far from where Mary Rogers's body had been found. On August 25, 1841, two of Loss's young sons, who had been playing in the woods, found various articles of women's clothing, including a handkerchief with the initials "M.R." on it. Mrs. Loss immediately notified the police of her sons' findings

This new discovery ignited an investigation by the New Jersey police, since they now decided Rogers had indeed been killed in

New Jersey. However, nothing became of the investigation and it soon ended.

Throughout the years, several criminologists tried to explain who killed Mary Rogers, and why. Yet no credible evidence has ever materialized and no one was ever charged with the crime.

A year after Rogers's death, Edgar Allen Poe, obviously saddened by the tragedy of "The Beautiful Cigar Girl," wrote his famous novel, "The Mystery of Marie Roget." The novel was set in Paris, and it duplicated the events that had occurred surrounding Rogers's death. In the novel, Poe's famous detective, Austin Dupin, concluded that the murderer was a naval officer of dark complexion, who had previously attempted to elope with Marie (Rogers), which explained her first disappearance in 1838. This mysterious Naval officer then killed Rogers in 1841 after she refused to marry him a second time.

Poe's novel closely mirrored the most credible explanation of Mary Rogers's death, which was put forth by author Raymond Paul in the early 1970s. Paul's theory was that Daniel Payne had murdered Rogers, but not on the Sunday she disappeared (for which Payne had a solid alibi), but on the following Tuesday. Because Rogers's body was still in rigor mortis when she was found, she could not have been dead for more than 24 hours. Rigor mortis starts scant hours after a person dies, but then after 24 hours it gradually dissipates.

Paul concluded, from the evidence compiled more than 130 years earlier, that Payne had gotten Rogers pregnant, and on Sunday July 25, 1841, he ferried her off to Hoboken to have an abortion. While her mother and former fiancée were looking for Rogers, Rogers was recuperating from the abortion in a Hoboken inn.

Payne then returned to Hoboken on Tuesday, July 27, to pick up Rogers and bring her back to New York City. When Rogers told Payne she was breaking off their relationship, Paul concluded Payne strangled Rogers, and then dropped her body into the Hudson River. Paul also deduced from the circumstances that Rogers's brief disappearance in 1838 was for the same reason: to have an abortion.

After Rogers's death, Payne started drinking heavily. On October 7, 1841, Payne, after making the rounds of several New York City bars, purchased the poison laudanum. He took the ferry to Hoboken, and then went to Nick Moore's House, where he got properly drunk. Soused, Payne staggered, holding a bottle of brandy, to the very spot in the woods where Rogers's clothing had been found.

There, Payne wrote on a piece of paper, "To the world, here I am on the very spot. May God forgive me for my misspent life."

Payne put the note in his pocket, drank the laudanum, and washed it down with the brandy. Then he laid down and died.

The newspapers, and the New York City police, thinking Rogers had been killed on Sunday, for which Payne had an airtight alibi, figured Payne had committed suicide because the love of his life had been murdered. Yet, the police investigation had been so cursory, incomplete, and totally inefficient, they never considered the fact that it was impossible for Rogers to have been killed four days before she was found, because her body was still in the state of rigor mortis.

Although the murder of Mary Rogers has never officially been solved, her death was not in vain. The complete incompetency of the New York City police force, combined with pressure from an outraged New York City press and populace, compelled the city to totally revamp its policing procedures.

Starting in 1845, Watchmen and Roundsmen became obsolete, as New York City finally created a police force, comprised of men specifically trained to prevent and investigate crimes.

The Murder of the Crew of the E.A. Johnson by Albert Hicks - 1860

Albert E. Hicks, called "Hicksey" by his pals (if he had any) and "Pirate Hicks" by the police, was the last man to be executed for piracy in the United States of America.

Hicks was a freelance gangster, who lived with his wife and son at 129 Cedar Street in downtown Manhattan, only two blocks from the East River. Hicks felt his criminal enterprises were better served if he worked alone, and as a result, Hicks never joined any of the other gangs that prowled the waterfront in the treacherous 4th Ward. Working solo, the police suspected Hicks committed scores of robberies and over a dozen murders.

However, Hicks scoffed at that notion. "Suspecting it and proving it are two different things," he said.

In March 1860, Hicks tied on a big one at a Water Street dive, and he became so drunk, he could not walk the two blocks home. Instead, he staggered into a Cherry Street lodging house, figuring he'd sleep until he was sober enough to walk the rest of the way home. The owner of the establishment was a known crimp, or a man who specialized in shanghaiing, which was the practice of "kidnapping men into duty as sailors on ships, against their will, by devious techniques such as trickery, intimidation, or violence." Hicks asked the crimp for a nightcap, and that he got, as the crimp, not aware of Hicks' reputation, laced Hicks' rum with laudanum, which is an alcohol solution containing opium.

The nightcap knocked Hicks out cold and when he awoke the next morning, he found himself at sea, on the ship the *E. A. Johnson*," which was bound for Deep Creek, Virginia, to pick up a load of oysters. Five days later, the *E. A. Johnson* was found abandoned at sea, a few miles off the coast of Staten Island. The ship seemed to have ided with another vessel, and when it was finally secured, Coroner Schirmer and Captain Weed of the Second Precinct Police Station, boarded the boat to examine the cause of its condition. No one was on board, but in the ship's cabin they found the room ransacked, and the floor, ceiling, and bunks filled with blood. On the deck, they found four human fingers and a thumb lying under the rail.

The next day, two residents of the Cedar Street house, where Hicks lived with this family, told the police that Hicks had returned home with a considerable sum of money, and was now gone, with no trace of him, or his family. In fact, Hicks had packed his belongings and escaped with his family to a boarding house in Providence, Rhode Island.

New York City Patrolman Nevins traced Hicks, and with the help of the Providence police, he arrested Hicks's entire family. When Patrolman Nevins searched Hicks's belongings, he found a watch and a daguerreotype (an early version of a camera), which belonged to Captain Burr, the captain of the *E. A. Johnson*. The two other missing seamen were brothers, Smith and Oliver Watts, but nothing could be found belonging to them and their fate remained a mystery.

As a result, Hicks was arrested and locked up in the Tombs Prison. At his trial in May, it took the jury only seven minutes to convict Hicks of piracy and murder on the high seas. He was sentenced to be hanged at Bedloe's Island on Friday the 13th, which was certainly a double-bad-luck day for Hicks.

A week after his trial, Hicks decided to become downright chatty. Hicks summoned the warden and several newspapermen to his cell, and he began spilling the beans about the whole sordid affair.

"I was brooding about being shanghaied," Hicks said "And I decided to avenge myself by murdering all hands on the ship."

Hicks told the assembled crowd that he was steering the ship, while Captain Burr and one of the Watts brothers was sleeping in the cabin below. The other Watts brother was on lookout at the bow. Hicks lashed the steering wheel to keep the ship on course, then he picked up an iron bar, sneaked to the bow of the ship, and hit the lookout over the head with the bar, knocking him out cold.

The other Watts brother heard the noise, and he rushed topside. By this time, Hicks had found an ax, and when the boy climbed onto the deck, Hicks decapitated him with one mighty blow. Hicks then rushed down to the cabin and confronted Captain Burr, who had just awakened from a deep sleep. The Captain put up a brave battle, but in the end, he too was decapitated.

Hicks said he then heard rumblings from up top. Hicks rushed up to the deck, and he found the first Watts boy staggering around in obvious pain. Hicks knocked him down with a heavy blow. Then he picked him up, carried him to the rail and tried to throw the boy overboard. The boy clutched at the railing, and Hicks used the ax to chop off the boy's five fingers, after which the lad toppled into the murky waters below.

Hicks threw the other two bodies overboard. Then he rushed below and ransacked the cabin, looking for money and valuables. When he saw the coast of Staten Island, Hicks lowered a small boat, and he rowed the rest of the way to land.

Hicks's confession made him an instant celebrity. Hundreds of gawkers paid the prison guards small fees to see Hicks shackled in his cell. And for a few pennies more, they were allowed to speak with the condemned man himself.

Among Hicks's many visitors was circus owner P.T. Barnum, who offered Hicks $25, a new suit of clothes, and two boxes of cigars, in exchange for a plaster cast of Hicks's head, which Barnum, the enterprising chap that he was, had planned to display in his circus, after Hicks's execution. Hicks agreed, but later on his way to the gallows, he complained to the warden that the suit was cheap and it did not fit properly. The warden told Hicks it was too late for alterations.

On the morning of July 13, Hicks, led my Marshall Rynders and a crowd estimated at 1500 people, started a procession to the docks. Rynders and Hicks boarded the boat accompanied by several policemen, and they sailed for Bedloe's Island, where a gallows had been erected 30 feet from the water. Hundreds of boats followed the doomed man, and it was estimated that 10,000 people came to witness Hicks's execution.

After the noose was slung around Hicks's neck and the ground removed from beneath his feet, Hicks struggled for a full three minutes before he stopped moving. Hicks was then cut down and pronounced dead.

Hicks was buried at Calvary Cemetery. However, a few days later, Hicks's body was stolen and sold to medical students, intent on studying the brain of a man who could commit such vile atrocities without much remorse.

The Murder of Albert Deane Richardson by Daniel McFarland - 1869

She was a famous New York City stage actress named Abby Sage. But after her ex-husband, Daniel McFarland, murdered her lover, journalist Albert Deane Richardson, it was Sage's lifestyle that was put on trial, not just McFarland.

Daniel McFarland was born in Ireland in 1820, but he immigrated to America with his parents when he was four-years-old. McFarland's parents died when he was 12, leaving him an orphan. Determined to make something of himself in America, McFarland worked at hard labor in a harness shop, saving his money so that he could attend college. By the time he was 17, McFarland had saved enough cash to attend a distinguished Ivy League university, Dartmouth. At Dartmouth, McFarland studied law, and he did extremely well. Upon graduation, McFarland passed the bar exam, but instead of practicing law, McFarland took a position at Brandywine college, teaching elocution, the skill of clear and expressive speech.

In 1853, McFarland traveled to Manchester, New Hampshire, where he met a beautiful 15-year-old girl named Abby Sage. Abby came from a poor but respectable family; her father was a weaver. However, Abby was quite bright, and soon she became a teacher as well as a published writer. Four years after they had met, McFarland and Abby Sage married. She was just 19; he was twice her age.

Later Abby wrote in an affidavit concerning McFarland's murder trial, "At the time of our marriage, Mr. McFarland represented to me that he had a flourishing law practice, brilliant political prospects, and property worth $30,000, but while on our bridal tour he was forced to borrow money in New York to enable us to proceed to Madison, Wisconsin, which was decided upon as our future home. We had resided in this town but a short time when he confessed that he had no law practice of any consequence, and that he had devoted himself solely to land speculation, some of which had resulted disastrously."

In February 1858, the married couple moved to New York City. McFarland told Abby that in New York City he had a better chance of selling the $20,000 to $30,000 worth of property he owned in Wisconsin. However, McFarland sold nothing at first, and soon Abby had to pawn most of her jewelry to pay the rent.

With the bills piling up and still no money coming in, McFarland figured it was better if he went at it alone. As a result, McFarland sent Abby back to her father's home in New Hampshire. In late 1858, McFarland was finally able to sell some of his Wisconsin properties. Soon after, he brought Abby back to New York City, and they settled in a rented cottage in Brooklyn. There their first son, Percy, was born in 1860, and a second son, Daniel, in 1864.

McFarland's land-selling business went flat, and he started drinking heavily.

Abby later wrote: "At first Mr. McFarland professed for me the most extravagant and passionate devotion, but soon he began to drink heavily, and before we were married a year, his breath and body were steaming with vile liquor. I implored him to reform, but he cried out: 'My brain is on fire and liquor makes me sleep.'"

At the start of the Civil War, the McFarlands briefly returned to Madison. Soon McFarland realized, under the right circumstances and with the right training, his beautiful, young wife could be the better wage-earner of the two. To implement his plan, the McFarlands traveled back to New York City in order to school Abby to become an actress.

In New York City, Abby tried her hand at dramatic readings, and she discovered she had a talent for the stage. One thing led to another, and soon Abby was acting in several plays and making the tidy sum of $25 a week. Abby's career advanced so quickly, soon she appeared opposite the great actor Edwin Booth in the *Merchant of Venice* (Edwin Booth was the older brother of John Wilkes Booth, the man who shot and killed Abraham Lincoln). Abby also supplemented her income by writing several articles about children and nature. She even penned a book of poetry entitled *Percy's Book of Rhymes*, after her son Percy.

Abby's artistic achievements allowed her to increase her circle of friends. She became fast pals with newspaper magnate Horace Greeley, his sister Mrs. John Cleveland, and *New York Tribune* publisher Samuel Sinclair and his wife.

However, his wife's successes did nothing to placate the wild nature of McFarland. He used his wife's new friends and their connections to get himself a political appointment.

Abby later said, "Through the influence of Horace Greeley, founder of the *New York Tribune*, I procured a position for him (McFarland) with one of the Provost marshals."

Soon, McFarland became jealous of Abby's new friends and his drinking increased exponentially. McFarland kept the money Abby made from her acting and writing, and he spent it all on booze. McFarland started opening Abby's private mail, and if he didn't like what he read, he would threaten to kill Abby and himself.

"By this time he had become a demon," Abby said. "He would rise in bed, tear the bed clothing into shreds and threaten to kill me. When he became exhausted, he would tearfully beg my pardon and go to sleep."

One time McFarland became so enraged, he struck Abby in the face, so hard, it caused her to stumble backwards. From that point on, their relationship changed dramatically.

"There was a look in his eyes that made him burst into a paroxysm of tears and to beg wildly that I should forgive him," Abby said. "But from that moment, I could never tell him that I loved him or forgave him, because it would not have been the truth."

In January 1867, the McFarlands moved into a boarding house at 72 Amity Street in New York City. Soon after, Albert Deane Richardson, who was in his mid-30's at the time, moved into the same boarding house. Richardson was already known to Abby, since they had met at the home of Mr. and Mrs. Sinclair. Richardson had an orange-colored beard and hazel eyes, and was considered to be a very distinguished-looking individual of the highest character.

Richardson, born in Massachusetts, was one of the most famous reporters of his time. He was well known for his writings as a war correspondent for the *New York Tribune* during the Civil War, and he also spent time acting as a spy for the Northern army.

In 1862, Richardson was captured by the South at Vicksburg, and he spent a year and a half in two separate Confederate prisons. In December 1863, while imprisoned in Salisbury, North Carolina, Richardson and another war correspondent escaped from prison and traveled four hundred miles on foot, until they reached the Union lines in Knoxville.

At the time of his imprisonment, Richardson had a wife and four children. When he returned home, he discovered his wife and infant daughter had died. Richardson assumed the support and care of his three other children, which at the time of his death, were 13, 10, and 6.

Back at his desk at the *New York Tribune*, Richardson capitalized on his Civil War heroics by writing about his escape. The title of his newspaper article was *Out of the Jaws of Death and Out of the Mouth of Hell.* It was considered one of the finest pieces of journalism that came out of Civil War era.

Richardson expanded this article into a book, and combined with his other writings, Richardson had transformed himself from a war prisoner into a wealthy man. So much so, Richardson bought shares in the *New York Tribune*, making himself a minority owner of the newspaper.

At the time he moved into the same boarding house as the McFarlands, Richardson was now an editor/writer for the *New York Tribune*. (Author's note: I was a sports columnist for the reincarnation of the *New York Tribune* in the 1980s.) Richardson used his room at 72 Amity Street as an office as well as a place to sleep. As his staff at 72 Amity Street, Richardson employed a stenographer, an artist, and a messenger boy to deliver his work to the *New York Tribune* offices downtown on Park Row.

On February 19, 1867, McFarland returned to the boarding house, and he found his wife standing outside Richardson's door. Abby claimed Richardson and her were discussing one of his articles, but McFarland would have none of that.

Abby later wrote: "When we entered our apartment, my husband flew into a rage and insisted that an improper intimacy existed between Mr. Richardson and I."

McFarland immediately went on a three-day bender, during which he again threatened Abby's life and said he would commit suicide. Finally, on February 21, Abby left McFarland for good. She grabbed her two children and took up residence with Mr. and Mrs. Samuel Sinclair.

At the Sinclairs, Abby summoned her father, who now lived in Massachusetts, and she enlightened him as to her marital situation. It was agreed upon that McFarland would be invited to the Sinclair residence. When McFarland arrived, Abby, in the presence of the Sinclairs and her father, told McFarland that their marriage was over.

That same evening Richardson called at the Sinclair residence. Richardson offered Abby his condolences and said he would do anything he could do to help her in her time of need. Then, as he was leaving, Abby followed him out to the hallway.

With tears in her eyes she said: "You have been very kind to me. I cannot repay you."

Referring to Abby's two children, Richardson said, "How do you feel about facing the world with two babies?"

She answered, "It looks hard for a woman, but I am sure I can get on better without that man than with him."

Before leaving, Richardson told Abby, "I wish you to remember, that any responsibility you choose to give me in any possible future, I shall be glad to take."

Two days later, Richardson asked Abby to marry him, telling her that he wanted to give her his motherless children for her to care for as she would her own.

Abby later said, "It was absolutely impossible for me not to love him."

On the night of March 13, 1867, Richardson met Abby at the theater where she had just finished a performance. As they turned a corner, McFarland rushed up behind them and fired three shots, one of which pierced Richardson's thigh. It was a superficial wound, and Richardson was not badly hurt. McFarland was arrested by the police, but due to some inexplicable courthouse dealings, McFarland somehow managed to escape jail time.

When it was obvious to McFarland that his wife was lost to him forever, he decided to sue to get custody of both their children. The courts came to a split decision, whereby Abby would get custody of Daniel and McFarland the custody of Percy. In April 1868, Abby attempted to see her son Percy, but she was denied doing so by McFarland, who flew into a rage and threatened to hit her. At this point, Abby had no choice but to file for divorce.

In the state of New York, the only grounds for divorce was adultery. So, in July of 1868, Abby decided to go to Indiana for her divorce, where the grounds for divorce were more extensive. Those grounds included drunkenness, extreme cruelty, and failure to support a wife. Abby stayed in Indiana for 16 months until her divorce from McFarland was final. Then Abby traveled to her family's home in Massachusetts, and Richardson met her there to spend Thanksgiving Day 1869 with her and her family.

On November 25, 1869, at 5:15 p.m., McFarland walked into the Park Row offices of the *New York Tribune*. He hid quietly in a corner for about 15 minutes until he saw Richardson enter through the side entrance on Spruce Street. While Richardson was reading his mail at the counter, McFarland rushed up to him and fired several shots. Richardson was hit three times, but he was still able to walk up two flights of stairs to the editorial office, where he flung himself on the couch, mortally wounded with a bullet in the chest. When the medics arrived, Richardson was carried across City Hall to the Astor House and laid down on a bed in room 115.

At 10 p.m., McFarland was arrested in room 31 of the Westmoreland Hotel, on the corner of 17th Street and Fourth Avenue. The arresting officer, Captain A. J. Allaire, told McFarland he was under arrest for the shooting of Richardson. At first, McFarland said he was innocent of the charges.

Then he shockingly said, "It must have been me."

Captain Allaire took McFarland into custody and brought him to the Astor House, room 115. After Captain Allaire asked Richardson if the man in front of him had been his attacker, Richardson rose his head off the pillow weakly and said, "That is the man!'

Abby Sage was immediately summoned to New York City. As soon as she arrived, at Richardson's request, arrangements were made by Horace Greeley so that Abby and Richardson could be married at Richardson's deathbed. The marriage ceremony was performed by Rev. Henry Ward Beecher and the Rev. O.B. Frothingham. Three days later on December 2, Richardson took his last breath, leaving Abby Sage Richardson a widow.

Before McFarland's trial, his defense attorney John Graham told the New York press that Abby Sage's intentions towards Mr. Richardson were anything but honorable.

Graham said, "This tender and touching marriage was a horrible and disgraceful ceremony to get the property of a dying man, and that tended to hasten his demise."

At first, Richardson's fellow New York City journalists defended the honor of Richardson, and they began delving into McFarland's life, trying to find anything that would discredit McFarland.

The *New York Tribune* wrote that McFarland was in "the habit of opium eating for the purpose of drowning his sorrows."

However, the *New York Sun* went on a campaign to discredit both Abby Sage and Richardson. In an editorial entitled *A Public Outrage on Religion and Decency*, the *Sun* accused Richardson of luring Abby away from her loving husband.

The *Sun* even dredged up a quote from McFarland's brother which said, "Abby went reading just to get a chance to paint her face, pass for beauty, and get in with that free-love tribe at Sam Sinclair's."

What followed was a battle in the press, where most of the New York City dailies opined that it was Richardson and Abby who were immoral, and that McFarland did the honorable thing in killing the man who had stolen his wife away from him.

McFarland's trial commenced on April 4, 1870. Since she knew her ex-husband's defense lawyer was on a mission to disgrace and discredit her, Abby stayed away from the trial. Yet Graham sought to secure sympathy from the jury towards his client by having McFarland's son, Percy, sitting next to him during the trial.

In his opening argument, Graham implored the jury to understand the mental anguish his client had been forced to endure.

Graham said, "So sensitive and tender was the defendant's mental organization that he was incapable of grappling with, and bearing the deep sorrows and misfortune that awaited him. His speculations were disastrous and then the seeds of dissatisfaction first began to be sown."

Graham got to the main thrust of his defense, when he attacked the virtue and honor of Abby Sage.

"When she first met my client, she was but a poor factory girl. Yet on one occasion she told my client, 'All I need to make me an elegant lady and popular with the elite of New York is money.' "

Graham then told the jury that the turning point in his client's life came on February 21, 1867, when McFarland arrived home at 3 p.m. and saw his wife exiting Richardson's room.

"This beautiful woman was completely corrupted," Graham said. "She had placed before her as temptations the honors of the stage and the society of great men. She was then too elegant and too popular for her humble lot, and the demon that placed her before all these temptations for which she must pay the price with her soul was Richardson."

Graham pointed out that the boiling point for his client had been reached one day when McFarland went to the office of the *New York Tribune.* There he was given a letter by an office boy that was addressed to "Mrs. McFarland." The boy had mistakenly thought the letter was addressed to "*Mr.* McFarland."

Graham told the jury, "My client opened the letter, peruses it and finds it is a love letter written by Richardson, who was in Boston, to Mrs. McFarland. In this letter, Richardson openly claims his intentions to marry this woman if she can obtain a divorce from Mr. McFarland."

During the trial, the prosecutors, led by former judge and then-congressman, Noah Davis, concentrated on how McFarland, during his marriage, had mistreated his wife and on occasions beat her. To back up these claims, the prosecution called in Abby's relatives and friends, including a man of great clout, Horace Greeley.

However, Greeley was no fan of the corrupt Democratic machine Tammany Hall, whom Greeley excoriated many times in his newspaper. As payback, Tammany Hall used their considerable influence, before and during the trial, to discredit Greeley and Abby Sage.

In his summation to the jury, which took two days, Graham tried to sway the jury into thinking his client was just the victim of unbearable consequences.

"The evidence proves the insanity under which the defendant was laboring at the time of the shooting," Graham said. "This was a condition of mind superinduced by the agony he endured at the thought of the loss of his home, his wife, and his children."

Graham even went so far as to quote the Bible to discredit the dead Richardson.

With tears in his eyes, Graham said, "Whoso committeth adultery with a woman lacketh understanding; he that doeth it destroyeth his own soul. A wound and dishonor shall he get; and his reproach shall not be wiped away. For jealousy is the rage of a man; therefore he will not spare in the day of vengeance."

The jury bought Graham's incredible defense like a mark buys into a three-card-monte game. On May 10, it took the jury only one hour and 55 minutes to return a verdict of not-guilty on the grounds of insanity.

Although she was deeply despondent after the trial, Abby Sage

Richardson steadfastly remained in New York City. She became a successful author and playwright, and was well-received in both the literary and social communities. She also edited and published a book of Richardson's unpublished works.

Abby also kept her promise to the dying Richardson that she would raise his three children as her own. She also raised her son Daniel, whose name was changed to Willie (not to be associated with his father Daniel McFarland). Abby's other son, Percy, left McFarland and returned to his mother. He changed his surname from McFarland to his mother's maiden name of Sage.

On December 5, 1900, Abby Sage Richardson died in Rome of pneumonia.

In 1880, Daniel McFarland traveled out west. He was last heard from in Colorado, and there is no recorded account of his death.

However, according to historian Edmund Pearson, "It did not take him long to drink himself to death."

Albert Richardson was buried in his home town of Franklin, Mass. Prominently displayed at Franklin's City Hall is a monument to Richardson's heroics in the Civil War.

The inscription on the monument reads: "Many give thee thanks who never knew thy face, so, then, farewell, kind heart and true."

The Murder of William Dunn by William J. Sharkey - 1872

He was a crook, a pickpocket, a Tammany Hall politician, and finally - a murderer. Yet William J. Sharkey was best known for his daring escape from death row in New York City's Tombs Prison, while he awaited execution for the murder of fellow gambler William Dunn..

Sharkey was born in New York City in 1845, to a well-to-do family which resided in the Ninth Ward in Manhattan. Despite the affluence of his family, Sharkey gravitated to the dark side. He began hanging out with pickpockets, gamblers, and crooks, and soon he became a very capable pickpocket himself and a gambler of some renown. Sharkey was eventually arrested for pickpocketing, and he had his picture taken by the municipal photographer, giving himself a definitive presence in the criminal records section of New York City Police Department.

Dealing in stolen bonds, Sharkey soon climbed the criminal ladder. With the money from his illicit endeavors piling in, Sharkey formed his own gang called "Sharkey's Guards," which had their headquarters at the corner of Wooster and Houston Streets.

It was there that Sharkey insinuated himself into the local political scene, and soon he was the darling of the crooks who ran Tammany Hall. Sharkey dressed in the finest clothes, wearing sparkling diamonds on his fingers and around his neck. Soon, Tammany Hall put Sharkey up for election for Assistant Alderman. Even though Tammany Hall had influence and muscle working in their favor at the polls, Sharkey somehow lost the election. Disappointed with his political failure, Sharkey decided to go back to his first loves: stealing and gambling.

With the money he made from various illegal endeavors, Sharkey traveled to Buffalo, New York, and he started a faro game. However, Sharkey was so unlucky, he managed to lose $4,000 in just five days. Downtrodden, Sharkey returned to New York City, and he hooked up with his old friend Robert Dunn, real name Bob Isaacs.

Dunn was an employee of the City's Comptroller's Office, but he was also a faro dealer in a Fulton Street gambling house. Figuring Dunn was a more capable faro player than he, Sharkey gave Dunn

$600, and he told him to go to Buffalo and try his hand at faro. Dunn agreed that if he was successful in Buffalo, he promised to repay Sharkey the $600 plus half his winnings.

As luck would have it, Dunn was just as unlucky in Buffalo as Sharkey, and he lost his entire stake. Dunn returned to New York City, and he told Sharkey the bad news.

On September 1, 1872, Dunn and Sharkey attended the funeral of James Riley, a prominent member of the Michael Norton Association, a political arm of Tammany Hall. After the funeral, Sharkey and Dunn traveled separately to a saloon owned by Charles Harvey, called "The Place," located at 288 Hudson Street.

By the time Sharkey had arrived, Dunn had already imbibed a few rye whiskeys at the bar. Sharkey ordered a rye himself, and after he knocked it down in one gulp, Sharkey demanded his $600 back from Dunn. Dunn told Sharkey he was tapped out himself, and he couldn't repay the money. Sharkey immediately drew a single-shot Derringer pistol, and he pointed it at Dunn's chest.

Dunn screamed, "Don't shoot, Billy! I'll pay you as soon as I can!"

Sharkey would have none of that. He bellowed back, "You better pay me now!"

Before Dunn could reply, Sharkey fired the Derringer point-blank at Dunn. The bullet pierced Dunn's heart, killing him instantly. Sharkey fled the scene of the crime, but he was captured a few hours later in a boarding house on Washington Street, near Perry Street.

Sharkey was tried, convicted, and sentenced to be hanged at the Tombs Prison, on August 15, 1873. However, Sharkey's connections at Tammany Hall pushed back his execution date to early December.

While Sharkey was imprisoned, he was visited daily by the most beautiful Maggie Jourdan, herself a very successful pickpocket. Miss Jourdan arrived at the prison early every morning, and she always stayed until visiting hours were over. Miss Jourdan was a great friend of Mrs. Wesley Allen, the wife of a burglar, whose brother, John Allen, owned a bawdy dance hall on Water Street. John Allen was known as "The Wickedest Man in New York City."

While most prisoners at the Tombs lived in perpetual squalor, Sharkey lived quite nicely on the second tier of the prison in an area called "Murderer's Row." With the money Jourdan earned stealing, and also by her hocking her jewelry including her gold watch,

Sharkey was able to decorate his jail cell No. 40 (which was never locked) with the finest furniture. Jordan bought Sharkey a walnut table, a Kidderminster carpet, a canary in a cage, and a book-and-magazine rack, which was suspended from the ceiling by silken cords. Jourdan also supplied Sharkey with a soft mattress for his bed, a comfortable chair for his lounging, draperies for his cell door, an elegant dressing gown made of velvet and cherry-colored silk, and velvet slippers.

Jourdan often told Sharkey during her visits, that if he died, she no longer wanted to live.

"Willie, I could never let you suffer," she tearfully told him.

On November 19, 1873, at exactly 10 a.m., Jourdan arrived at the Franklin Street entrance of The Tombs. The guard on duty gave her the usual pass given to all visitors. The bottom part of her body was noticeably bulky, but the prison guards thought she had just put on additional petticoats to protect herself the from the cold November air. Jourdan immediately went to Sharkey's cell, and she spoke to him for several hours. The prison guards were so accustomed to her being there, they hardly paid any attention to what she did, or what she said to Sharkey.

Mrs. Wesley Allen arrived at the prison at 12:30 p.m. She stopped at Sharkey's cell on the second tier, and she spoke to both Jourdan and Sharkey. Then Mrs. Allen went upstairs to the third tier to visit a prisoner named Flood. At 1 p.m., Jourdan exited the prison, which was quite unusual, since she always stayed until the end of the day.

A half an hour later, a strange-looking woman, with especially broad shoulders, walked down the second-tier corridor, through two lower gates and out of the prison. As this dubious lady exited the prison, she handed her pass to the guard minding the exit. This woman wore a heavy black woolen dress, a black coat, an Alpine bonnet, and a thick green veil which covered her entire face. Patrolmen Dolan was walking down Franklin Street, when he saw this woman jump nimbly onto a passing streetcar, even though she was wearing high French heels.

At 2:05 p.m., Mrs. Wesley Allen tried to exit the prison. As she passed the guard standing at the exit, the guard asked her for her visitor's pass. Mrs. Allen nervously fumbled in her dress pockets for several seconds before she said, "I put it in my pocket, but I must have lost it."

The guard, realizing something was up, immediately summoned Warden Johnson. Mrs. Allen was detained, while Warden Johnson ordered all cells in the prison to be immediately searched. During this search, they were dismayed to discover that Sharkey's cell was empty. His elegant clothes were scattered about his cell, and right above his washbasin were the remnants of his flowing mustache, which had obviously just been shaved off.

Mrs. Allen was immediately arrested, but since there was no concrete evidence to incriminate her, the police reluctantly released her. Jourdan was arrested that night at her mother's home at 167 Ninth Ave. When the detectives told her she was under arrest, Jourdan replied, "I am the happiest little woman in the world."

Jourdan was tried in General Sessions Court, and she was defended by the infamous attorney, Big Bill Howe. Howe was so efficient in Jourdan's defense, the jury acquitted her on all charges.

It was later determined, that despite the fact the police had searched all the piers in the city looking for Sharkey, Sharkey had escaped on the schooner *Frank Atwood,* and had made his way to Haiti. Not liking that country too much, Sharkey boarded another boat, and he traveled to Cuba, where he settled.

Two years after Sharkey had made his escape from The Tombs Prison, Maggie Jourdan joined Sharkey in Cuba. However, for some unknown reason (probably because Sharkey was an incorrigible creature), Sharkey badly mistreated Jourdan; the very woman responsible for Sharkey avoiding the gallows in New York City. Sharkey abused Jourdan so much, the captain of the ship who had taken Jourdan to Cuba, hustled her back on board and took her back to New York City.

Soon afterwards, Jourdan found her true love, whom she married. They presumably lived happily ever after.

As far as it can be determined, William J. Sharkey never returned to New York City.

The Murder of Architect Stanford White by Harry Kendall Thaw - 1906

One was a world-famous architect, and the other a rich scion from an even richer family. There are no nice guys involved here and the girl in the middle, although she was considered the most beautiful woman of her time and one of artist Charles Dana Gibson's famous "Gibson Girls," was no lily-white lassie herself.

So why do we care? Simply because it was the most deliciously decadent murder story of the early 20th Century.

On June 25, 1906, it was high society's night out. It was the opening of the new musical *Mamzelle Champagne*, on the outdoor roof garden of Madison Square Garden, which at the time was bounded by Fifth and Madison Avenues, and 26th and 27th Streets. The structure, which included an amphitheater on the ground floor, was designed by world-famed architect Stanford White. In fact, White had a front-row table that night, where he sat by himself to enjoy the show, which was not going over too well with the crowd, since people were milling about from table to table, kibitzing, instead of paying attention to the festivities.

Suddenly, the audience heard three loud shots. At first, they thought it was a part of the show. But when they saw White topple to the floor, his head encased in a pool of blood, they knew this scene was for real.

Harry Kendall Thaw, a spoiled, rich punk, had casually walked over to White, pulled out a pistol from beneath his long black coat, and plugged White three times, twice in the shoulder and once through his brain.

After he fired his final shot, Thaw screamed at White, "You deserved this! You ruined my wife!"

Seeming to not be in any particular hurry, Thaw casually pointed the gun up over his head, and he strode to the elevator. Thaw took the elevator down and joined his wife, the beautiful actress Evelyn Nesbit, in the lobby by the elevator.

Because *Mamzelle Champagn* was quite unentertaining, Thaw and Nesbit had left with another couple moments before the shooting. Nesbit did not realize her husband did not ride down the elevator with her. Nesbit heard the shots, and a few seconds later, when her husband strode out of the elevator holding a smoking gun, she screamed, "Good God Harry, what have you done?"

Back on the rooftop garden, the stage manager was trying to sort out exactly what had transpired. He jumped on a table and shouted to the orchestra, "Keep on playing! And bring out the chorus!"

The musicians, actors, and actresses, dumbfounded over a real-life murder being perpetrated right in front of their eyes, sat or stood dumbfounded. A doctor who was in attendance rushed to White's body. White's face had been disfigured from the powder burns, and the doctor announced with great certainty that White was indeed dead.

Down in the lobby, a fireman in attendance wrestled the gun away from Thaw, who did not offer much resistance. Moments later, a policeman arrived, and he immediately arrested Thaw. The policeman brought Thaw to the nearest police station, which was located in the Tenderloin District, an area known for its gambling, prostitution, and various other crimes, both violent and non-violent. When Thaw arrived at the police station, he identified himself as John Smith, a student at 18 Lafayette Square in Philadelphia.

The desk sergeant asked Thaw, "Why did you do this?"

Thaw seemed disinterested. "I can't say why," he said.

By this time, several news reporters, who were familiar with Thaw, had followed him to the police station, and they identified him to the police by his real name. Thaw immediately clammed up, and he refused to say another word unless he was represented by an attorney.

The following day, the killing of Stanford White was on the front page of every newspaper in New York City. The *New York Times*, usually staid and proper, ran this blaring headline:

THAW MURDERS STANFORD WHITE!
Shoots him on the Madison Square Garden rooftop
ABOUT EVELYN NESBIT
"You ruined my wife," he cries and fires.
AUDIENCE IN PANIC
Chairs and tables overturned in a wild scramble
For the Exits

Stanford White, who was born in 1853, was the most famous architect of his time. White was a partner in the architectural firm of McKim, Mead, and White, for which he designed houses and mansions for the rich and famous. White also designed the upscale gated community, Seagate, in Brooklyn. Besides designing Madison Square Garden, White also designed the Madison Square Presbyterian Church, the New York Herald Building, the First Bowery Savings Bank (at Bowery and Grand Street), and the Washington Square Arch. The final two White achievements still stand to this day.

However White, despite his exalted status, was a quirky man who had several fetishes, some bordering on illegal. Even though he was married, White was a man-about-town, who courted several young ladies, most of them young enough to be his daughter. It was his encounter with a 16-year-old Evelyn Nesbit that was the cause of his demise.

Evelyn Nesbit was born Florence Evelyn Nesbit on Christmas Day 1884, in Pittsburgh Pennsylvania. Her father was a struggling lawyer, who died in 1893 leaving his wife and daughter in considerable debt.

Even at a young age, Nesbit was a stunning beauty. She began modeling in Pittsburgh, but she and her mother decided it was best they move to New York City to enhance her modeling career. Almost immediately, Nesbit became a hot New York City item. She modeled for such famous photographers such as Frederick S. Church, Herbert Morgan, Gertrude Kasebier, Carl Blenner, and Rudolf Eickemeyer.

Nesbit's beauty was such, newspaperman Irvin S. Cobb described Nesbit as having, "The slim, quick grace of a fawn, a head that sat on her flawless throat like a lily on its stem, eyes that were the color of blue-brown pansies and the size of half dollars, a mouth made of rumbled rose petals."

In 1901, Nesbit met White for the first time. Nesbit and a girlfriend, who was accompanied by another man, were invited to have lunch at White's apartment on W. 24th Street. Shortly after they finished their meal, Nesbit's girlfriend's male companion left. White then invited the two girls to an upstairs room, where he kept a red velvet swing. Like a father doting on his two young children, White gave both girls a turn on his swing, gleefully pushing them back and forth, until their legs almost touched the ceiling.

"He had a big Japanese umbrella on the ceiling," Nesbit said. "So when he swung us very high up in the air, our feet passed through the umbrella."

White became smitten with Nesbit. Using her mother as a chaperon, White dated Nesbit quite often. During this time, White was the perfect gentleman, and he tried to make sure Nesbit had every advantage as she pursued her career in modeling and in acting.

However, everything changed when Nesbit's mother decided to visit friends in Pittsburgh. White was so magnanimous, he even paid for Nesbit's mother's trip. By this time, Nesbit had gotten a bit part in the play *Floradora*. On the second night that her mother was gone, White sent Nesbit a note at the theater, inviting her to a party at his apartment on W 24th Street. When Nesbit arrived at White's apartment, she was surprised no one else was there.

"The others have turned us down," White told Nesbit.

"Then he poured me a glass of champagne," Nesbit said at Thaw's trial. "I don't know whether it was a minute after, or two minutes after, but a pounding began in my ears. Then the whole room seemed to go around."

Nesbit lost consciousness, and when she awoke, she was lying in bed, naked. The room, in which the bed was located, was completely mirrored, even on the ceilings.

"I started to scream," Nesbit said. "Mr. White tried to quiet me. I don't remember how I got my clothes on, or how I went home, but he took me home. Then he went away and left me. I sat up all night."

The following day, White visited Nesbit at her apartment. He found her there in an almost hypnotic state, just staring out the window.

"Why don't you look at me, child?" White said.

"Because I can't," she said.

White told Nesbit not to worry. "Everyone does those things," he told her.

White also told Nesbit her fellow starlets in Floradora all were involved in sexual escapades with assorted men. White told Nesbit the most important thing was not to be found out. He made Nesbit promise not to say anything to her mother about what had transpired in his apartment the night before.

Harry Thaw was born in Pittsburgh in February 1871, the son of coal and railroad baron William Thaw. As a child, Thaw shuttled in and out of several schools. He was an insolent child, considered by his teachers not to be very bright and a troublemaker.

Yet, because he was the son of William Thaw, Harry Thaw was admitted into the University of Pittsburgh, supposedly to study law. However, Thaw was not much of a ege student, so his father used his influence to get him transferred to Harvard University. At Harvard, Thaw did little more than drink, carouse with the ladies, and play nightlong poker games.

Thaw left Harvard without a degree, and he became an expert at getting into trouble. It was about this time that Thaw began his systematic drug use. Thaw consumed large amounts of cocaine and heroin, and it was rumored that Thaw was heavy into "speedballing," which was the process of injecting a combination of cocaine and heroin into a vein.

High as a kite, Thaw once rode a horse into a New York City nightclub from which he had been banned. Adding to his reputation of being an out-of-control lunatic, Thaw also drove a car through a display window of a department store, lost $40,000 in a single poker game, drank a full bottle of the narcotic laudanum, and hosted a decadent party in Paris, where the majority of his guests were the top whores in town. The tab for this party was said to be more than $50,000.

When Thaw's father passed away, Thaw was dismayed to discover, that even though he was left $5 million of his father's $40 million estate, it was stipulated in the senior Thaw's will that his son would only get an allowance of $200 a month. This small allowance would continue until Thaw showed he was responsible enough to handle such a large sum of inheritance money.

In 1905, Thaw became smitten with Nesbit. Thaw courted Nesbit with much enthusiasm, and when White found out about Thaw and Nesbit, he warned Nesbit to stay away from Thaw; telling her that Thaw was an erratic and dangerous man. White knew that Thaw maintained a New York City apartment in a brothel. White also knew that Thaw enticed young girls into his apartment, where he would whip them in a bizarre sex routine that left the girls in conditions that would sometimes require hospitalization.

However, Thaw could not be discouraged from pursuing Nesbit.

He repeatedly begged Nesbit to marry him, and she consistently refused.

While they were on a cruise together, Thaw became outraged when Nesbit again refused to marry him. In an act of a madman, Thaw whipped Nesbit like he did the other young girls in his New York City apartment. During this whipping, Nesbit confessed to Thaw about the manner in which he had lost her virginity to White. Thaw said he still loved her and wanted to marry her anyway. Despite the fact that Thaw had whipped her, and was certainly not of sound mind, Nesbit married Thaw on April 4, 1905.

After they were married, Thaw maintained an extreme hatred for Stanford White. So contemptuous of White because of what White had done to Nesbit, Thaw forbade his wife to even mention the name "Stanford White." Thaw insisted that Nesbit refer to White as, "The Bastard" or "The Beast." Yet, Nesbit, more often than not, simply referred to White as "B."

While Thaw was in prison awaiting trial for the murder of White, Thaw's mother, known in the newspapers as "Mother Thaw," was in England visiting her daughter, the Countess of Yarmouth. Upon hearing of her son's predicament, Mother Thaw announced that she was going back to the United States to help her son.

"I am prepared to pay one million dollars to save my son's life," Mother Thaw told the press.

Part of Mother Thaw's strategy was to use her considerable wealth to orchestrate a campaign in the press to discredit Stanford White. Suddenly, several newspapers began writing exposés on White, portraying him as a tyrannical abuser of young girls. Mother Thaw went so far as to hire a press agent to generate newspaper publicity detrimental to White and favorable to her son.

One particular story, Mother Thaw paid the press to print, was extremely damaging to White's credibility, decency, and honor (if he had any to start with).

It seemed White had become infatuated with a 15-year-old girl named Susie Johnson. White had met Johnson at a wild party, at which Johnson had sprung from a large cake, almost totally naked. That night, White fed Johnson enough champagne to render her quite drunk. When Johnson became so inebriated she was barely conscious, White took Johnson back to his apartment, and he did to her what he had done to Evelyn Nesbit. Soon after, White banished

Johnson from his apartment, and he threw her out into the street, totally broke.

As White pushed Johnson out his front door, he told Johnson, "Girls, if you are poor, stay in the safe factory, or in the kitchen."

Johnson lasted eight years hustling on the streets, before she died at the age of 23. She was buried in a pauper's grave.

In order to influence the New York City potential jury pool, Mother Thaw hired a playwright to write a play almost identical to the circumstances surrounding Harry Thaw, Stanford White, and Evelyn Nesbit. The play featured three characters named Harold Daw, Emeline Daw, and Stanford Black.

In the final scene of the play, Harold Daw proclaimed from his cell in The Tombs prison, "No jury on earth will send me to the chair, no matter what I have done, or what I have been, for killing the man who defamed my wife. That is the unwritten law made by men themselves, and upon its virtue I will stake my life."

Mother Thaw's money even made it into the hands of Rev. Charles A. Eaton, who had John D. Rockefeller as one of his parishioners. Rev. Eaton made an impassioned speech to his congregation defending Thaw's actions.

Rev. Eaton said, "It would be a good thing if there was a little more shooting in cases like this."

While Thaw was in prison, his mother spread around enough money so that Thaw could enjoy extravagances no other prisoners in The Tombs were allowed. Instead of eating the standard prison grub, Thaw had all his meals delivered from Delmonico's, a downtown restaurant which was considered the finest eatery of its time. While other prisoners dressed in standard prison garb, Thaw was allowed to wear the finest clothes, including silk shirts and silk ties.

Thaw's first trial for the murder of Stanford White commenced on January 21, 1907. Mother Thaw hired the illustrious California trial lawyer, Delpin Delmas, to represent her son. District Attorney William Travers Jerome, the uncle of Winston Churchill, prosecuted the case for the state.

Jerome told the jury in his opening statement, "With all his millions, Thaw is a fiend. In the conduct of this trial, I shall prove that no matter how rich a man is, he can't get away with murder in New York County!"

The sensationalism of the trial was so extreme, tickets to the trial were scalped at $100. More than 80 world-famous artists and writers flocked to the courtroom to see if maybe they could benefit, from either writing a book or making a movie about the sordid affair.

The defense's shining hour was when Evelyn Nesbit took the stand in defense of her husband. Rumors had it that Mother Thaw had enticed Nesbit to testify by promising Nesbit that her son would agree to a divorce. Mother Thaw also promised Nesbit $1,000,000 after the trial. But Nesbit never received a penny of that money.

On the witness stand, Nesbit told of the bizarre sexual behavior of Stanford White. Nesbit said that White made her wear little girl's dresses when she came to his apartment. Nesbit also told the jury the manner in which she lost her virginity to White and that White had plied her with champagne in order to render her unconscious so that he could have his way with her

The prosecution countered Nesbit's words by eliciting testimony from a leading toxicologist, Dr. Rudolph Witthaus. Dr. Witthaus said that Nesbit's story about how White had gotten her drunk in order to take advantage of her did not hold water, because no drug known to science would have worked as rapidly as Nesbitt said the champagne did to render her unconscious.

Although a group of psychiatrists declared Thaw to be totally sane, during the trial Thaw acted erratically; constantly crying like a baby and flying into rages, in which his eyes bugged out and his face nearly turned purple.

In his final summation, Delmas told the jury that his client, when he shot Stanford White, had been consumed by "Dementia Americana, a form of insanity which makes every home sacred, makes a man believe that his wife is sacred. Whoever strains the virtual life has forfeited the protection of human laws, and must look to the internal justice and mercy of God."

Attorney Delmas had done such a remarkable job, the jury was not able to come to a unanimous verdict. It was revealed later that seven jurors had wanted to convict Thaw on a first-degree murder charge, while five jurors decided on a verdict of not guilty by reason of insanity. However, at Thaw's second trial, in January of 1908, the jury unanimously voted Thaw not guilty by reason of insanity.

Still, the verdict of not guilty did not set Thaw free from prison. Thaw was declared criminally insane and imprisoned for life at Mattawan, New York. In August 17, 1913, Thaw escaped, and with a limousine waiting for him outside the asylum, Thaw fled to Canada where he took refuge.

While Thaw was on the run, Nesbit, obviously angry at the fact she had not been paid the $1,000,000 she had been promised by Mother Thaw, made an announcement to the press.

She said, "Harry Thaw has turned out to be a degenerate scoundrel. He hid behind my skirts through two trials and I won't stand for it again. I won't let lawyers throw any more mud at me."

Soon afterwards, Nesbit signed a contract to appear in a vaudeville show at a salary of $3,500 a week.

In September of 1913, the United States government forced the Canadian Minister of Justice to return Thaw to the United States. Thaw faced a third trial in 1915. Bolstered by a cadre of the best lawyers money could buy, Thaw was found to be sane, and the jury found him not guilty of all charges.

Back on the streets, Thaw went back to his old, evil ways.

Eighteen months after he was released from prison, Thaw was arrested for kidnapping and whipping Frederick Gump. At his trial, Thaw was again declared insane. Yet, before Thaw went back into the asylum, he gave Nesbit her promised divorce. Nesbit spent the next decade appearing in vaudeville, occasional movies, and as a dancer in nightclubs throughout New York City.

In 1924, after seven years in the asylum, Thaw was finally declared sane, and he was released from prison. Thaw spent the rest of his life in and out of lucidity. Thaw died on February 22, 1947, at the age of 76, of a heart attack in Miami, Florida. Thaw left a mere $10,000 of his vast fortune to Evelyn Nesbit.

Nesbitt, beset by alcohol addiction, morphine addiction, and several suicide attempts, somehow lasted until January 17, 1967, when she died at the age of 82. Nesbit served as a technical advisor on the 1955 movie *The Girl in the Red Velvet Swing*, which was loosely based on her life story.

Marilyn Monroe was originally scheduled to play Evelyn Nesbit, but ultimately, she refused to play the part, which then went to Joan ins. Ray Milland played Stanford White and Farley Granger played Henry Thaw.

The Murder of Maxwell "Kid Twist "Zwerbach by Louie Pioggi

"Kid Twist," real name Maxwell Zwerbach, was a ruthless killer who rose up the ranks of the Monk Eastman mob, only to die because he decided to cheat on his wife.

Zwerbach was born in Austria in 1884. His Jewish father, Adolf, and half-Italian mother, Hanna, immigrated to New York City in 1886 to escape the anti-Semitic riots. The family took an apartment on Delancey Street, where Adolph opened a tailor shop. Adolph hoped his son would follow in his footsteps and alter clothes for a living. However, Zwerbach, who was now called Kid Twist on the mean streets of the Lower East Side, had other ideas.

Kid Twist started out as a petty thief. Soon, he hooked up with the famous Monk Eastman gang, made up of Jews who were constantly at war with Paul Kelly's (Paulo Vaccarelli) Italian Five Pointers over the Lower East Side rackets. Kid Twist killed his way up the ranks, until Eastman installed him as his top lieutenant, along with Richie Fitzpatrick, a Jewish killer who took on an Irish last name.

In early 1903, Eastman had the misfortune of getting himself locked up in a Freehold, New Jersey jail, after he beat up a potential witness against a friend of his on the courthouse steps. When Kid Twist heard of his boss's predicament, he rounded up 50 of his best thugs, with the intention of driving to New Jersey to bust Eastman out of jail.

However, before their cars could leave their Christie Street headquarters, a battalion of policemen, led by Inspector McCluskey, descended upon them and beat them with nightsticks back into their club.

Kid Twist decided to change tactics, and he contacted Eastman's cronies in Tammany Hall. The crooked pols used their Jersey connections and Eastman was sprung the following day.

Eastman was not so lucky in 1904, when he was arrested near Times Square for assault and robbery. This time Tammany Hall refused to come to his rescue. Eastman was tried, convicted, and sentenced to 10 years in the slammer.

Kid Twist thought he was now the rightful heir to Eastman's throne, but Fitzpatrick had the same idea. Both men argued over who was the new boss. Finally, Kid Twist told Fitzpatrick, he had a plan on how the rackets could be split down the middle with both men having separate but equal powers. Fitzpatrick thought Twist's idea sounded just swell, and he agreed to a meeting to work out the details.

On November 1, 1904, Kid Twist enticed Fitzpatrick into the back room of the Sheriff Street Saloon (which oddly enough, was located on Christie Street). As soon as Fitzpatrick arrived, the lights went out and so did Fitzpatrick. He was shot twice through the heart by Kid Dahl, real name Harris Stahl, thus installing Kid Twist as the No. 1 man in the Eastman Gang, all by himself.

As a result of Fitzpatrick's sudden demise, Kid Twist took over all of Eastman's operations, which included several brothels and stuss card games. In a show of bravado, Kid Twist announced to the world that "no Wop and no Mick would ever rule the Lower East Side of New York."

As a side moneymaker, Kid Twist championed his own brand of the popular "celery soda," which was the only brand of celery soda allowed to be sold on the entire Lower East Side of Manhattan.

Even though Kid Twist had several stuss games of his own, he coveted the one on Suffolk Street owned by the Bottler, which was under the protection of Paul Kelly's Five Pointers. First, Kid Twist approached the Bottler, and not in a very nice way, Kid Twist told him that he was now the Bottler's partner, not Paul Kelly. Before the ink was dry on Twist's verbal contract, he informed the Bottler that the Bottler was out completely, and that Kid Dahl was now Kid Twist's partner in the Suffolk Street stuss parlor.

This time the Bottler made a stand, and he refused to comply with Kid Twist's demands. As a result, Kid Twist imported Coney Islander Vach Lewis, known as Cyclone Louie, a professional circus strongman, who was famous for bending iron bars around his neck, and sometimes around other people's necks, too.

While Kid Twist was in the Delancey Street police station screaming at the desk sergeant over some trivial matter, and Kid Dahl was in a Houston Street restaurant arguing with the owner over what time of day it was, Cyclone Louie calmly walked into the Bottler's stuss parlor. As 20 customers looked on in shock, Cyclone

Louie shot the Bottler twice in the chest, killing him instantly.

With Kid Twist and Kid Dahl eliminated as suspects because of their contrived alibis, a few days later Kid Dahl strode into the Suffolk Street stuss parlor and announced to all that the stuss parlor was now his and Kid Twist's possession. All this did not please Paul Kelly too much, and he waited for the right time to get back what was rightfully his.

On the night of May 14, 1908, Kid Twist and Cyclone Louie decided to travel to Coney Island, to visit the supposedly happily married Kid Twist's girlfriend, dancer Carroll Terry. The two men were sitting inside the dance hall Terry performed in, when a kid rushed inside and told them Terry wanted to see them outside.

As soon as their feet hit the pavement, Kid Twist and Cyclone Louie were blasted with bullets fired by Kelly henchman, Louie "The Lump" Pioggi and several other of Kelly's men. It took only one slug to the brain, shot by Pioggi, to finish Kid Twist, but Cyclone Louie, true to his reputation as a strong man, needed five bullets in his torso to render him deceased.

When Terry showed up seconds later, Pioggi, a jilted suitor of hers, whipped a slug into her hip. Terry fell face forward, and although she would survive, the unconscious Terry landed across the body of her lifeless boyfriend, Maxwell "Kid Twist" Zwerbach, thereby putting a dent in the premise that "true love never dies."

The Murder of Big Jack Zelig by Red Davidson – 1912

Big Jack Zelig was born Zelig Harry Lefkowitz in New York City in 1888. Zelig started his criminal career at the age of nine. By the time Zelig had reached 13, and working for the Crazy Butch Gang on the Lower East Side, he became known as one of the best pickpockets in New York City. By the time he was 15, Zelig was a member of the feared Monk Eastman Gang. As an Eastman, Zelig was respected on the Lower East Side as a feared street fighter, who was especially adept at using a knife. Because of his roughhouse escapades, Zelig was dubbed by the police, "The Most Feared Man in New York City."

While Eastman was in jail for assault and robbery, the Eastman gang was headed by Max "Kid Twist" Zwerbach, who appointed Zelig his No. 1 lieutenant. When Zwerbach was killed in 1908 by a member of the rival Five Points Gang, Zelig took control of Zwerbach's gang.

Zelig's gang robbed casinos, banks and brothels, but their specialty was thuggery for hire. The Zelig gang even had a printed menu of the gang's services.

To have them slash the cheek of someone, it cost anywhere from $1 to $10, according to your ability to pay. A shot in the leg or arm cost $5 to $25. Tossing a live bomb to take down an establishment also cost $5 to $25. And to render someone dead, they charged anywhere from $10 to $100.

Zelig's capable men included such notables as Harry "Gyp the Blood" Horowitz, "Lefty" Louie Rosenberg, and "Dago Frank" Cirofisi.

Zelig's two chief nemeses, who were fighting with him behind the scenes for control of the former Eastman Gang, were gang members Chick Tricker and Jack Sirocco. Tricker and Sirocco tricked Zelig into going on a back robbery with them. After Tricker and Sirocco were in possession of the bank's cash, they left Zelig behind to take the rap. Zelig was arrested and none too happy with his pals.

To add insult to injury, Tricker and Sirocco refused to bail out Zelig; figuring with Zelig behind bars, they could assume control of his gang. However, Zelig had friends in high places in Tammany Hall, and soon he was set free. Thus commenced a war between Zelig, and Tricker and Sirocco.

On December 6, 1911, Zelig threw a shindig for his gang at Stuyvesant Hall. Tricker and Sirocco were not invited, but they sent their associate Jules Morello to the party, with the expressed intention of killing Zelig.

However, Morello had a few too many drinks at the bar, and he started yelling "Where's that Yid? I'm gonna kill that Yid."

Meaning Zelig.

Zelig heard the commotion, and before Morello could do him any damage, Zelig shot Morello four times, leaving him dead.

On October 15, 1912, Zelig was drinking at Segal's Cafe, at 76 Second Avenue, when he got a phone call from his girlfriend saying she needed company for the night. Delighted at his good fortune, Zelig hopped on the Second Avenue Street Car in front of Siegel's. When the street car reached 13th Street, a junkie thug named Red Davidson snuck up behind Zelig and shot him once behind the ear, killing him.

"The Most Feared Man in New York City" was now dead at the age of 24.

Davidson's motive was never ascertained, but it was reported Davidson killed Zelig because, a few days earlier, Zelig had beaten Davidson to a pulp over a monetary dispute.

The Murder of Albert Brown by Judd Gray and Ruth Brown Snyder -1927

One crime writer called it, "a cheap crime involving cheap people." Famous author and playwright Damon Runyon said the crime was so "idiotic," he coined it, "The Dumbbell Murders," because the murderers were so dumb.

Blond, broad-shouldered, and buxom, Ruth Brown Snyder was involved in a marriage she could no longer endure. Ruth told people her husband, Albert Snyder, 13 years her senior, had taken advantage of her youth and tricked her 10 years earlier, when she was only 19-years-old, into a marriage "she really didn't want." Snyder said Albert, an art editor with *Motor Boating Magazine*, was a mean man, who was able to convince her to marry him because she was young, innocent, and naïve. Snyder told people that on the day they were married, she was too weak and faint even to consummate the marriage with Albert.

Ruth Snyder said, "He had to wait till I was better before he got his way. But to him I was never any better than the ex-switchboard operator who worked in a typing pool."

Yet, after Albert's death, his editor and publisher, C. F. Chapman, said about Albert, "He was a man's man... a quiet, honest, upright man, ready to play his part in the drama of life without seeking the spotlight, or trying to fill the leading role. All the world is made up of good, solid, silent men like him."

Judd Gray was a nondescript, bespectacled corset salesman, who was also involved in a loveless marriage. According to Gray's coworkers, Gray's wife Isabel was an enigma. She was seldom seen or heard by anyone, and had taken on the aspect of an "invisible woman." Few of Gray's coworkers in the Bien Joilie Corset Company had ever met his wife, or had even spoken to her. In fact, some of his coworkers did not know that the 32-year-old Gray was married.

As he awaited the electric chair, Gray described his wife in his autobiography, as such: "Isabel, I suppose, one would call a home girl. She had never trained for a career of any kind. She was learning to cook, and was a careful and exceptionally exact housekeeper. As I think it over searchingly, I am not sure, and we were married these many years, of her ambitions, hopes, or her ideals. We made our home, drove our car, played bridge with our friends, danced, raised our child – ostensibly together – married. Never could I seem to attain with her the comradeship that formed the bond between my mother and myself."

It started out as a blind date arranged by another couple. Ruth Snyder and Judd Gray first met in a tiny restaurant in midtown Manhattan called "Henry's Swedish Restaurant." After four hours of complaining to each other about the miseries of their respective marriages, they vowed to meet again soon.

On August 4, 1925, Albert Snyder and his 7-year-old daughter Lorraine were on a boating trip to Shelter Island. Gray took this opportunity to knock on the door of the Snyder residence in Queens Village. Judd implored Ruth Snyder to have dinner with him at "their place": Henry's Swedish Restaurant. After they dined and imbibed more than a few alcoholic beverages, Gray invited Snyder to his office on 34th Street and Fifth Avenue. His excuse was, "I have to ect a case of sample corsets."

Inside Gray's office, Ruth complained to Gray that she had a bad sunburn. "I've got some camphor oil in my desk," Gray said. "Let me get it for you."

Gray retrieved the camphor oil, and he began rubbing the oil seductively on Ruth's reddened neck and shoulders, which aroused both people sexually. After the rubdown, Gray offered to give Snyder one of his new corsets, which he would graciously fit for her. Of course, this necessitated Ruth removing her blouse, which exposed her corpulent breasts. One thing led to another, and in the Bein Jolie Corset Company, Gray and Snyder first consummated their relationship. Ruth was so overcome with Gray's affections, she said to him, "Okay, from now on you can call me Momsie."

For the next 18 months, while Albert Snyder was at work, Ruth Snyder and Judd Gray met for numerous trysts in midtown hotels, or sometimes even at the Snyder residence. During these indiscretions, Ruth Snyder's daughter Lorraine was either downstairs sitting on the Snyder living room couch, or in the lobby of a sleazy Manhattan hotel. Their slobbering love affair was such that Gray frequently knelt at Snyder's feet, massaging her feet and ankles, declaring, "You are my Queen, my Momsie, my Mommie." Ruth would look down lovingly at Gray and say, "You are my baby, my 'Bud', my loverboy."

It was around this period of time, that Albert Snyder began having a series of strange "accidents." In the summer of 1925, Albert was jacking up his family Buick so that he could change a flat tire. Suddenly, the jack slipped and the car fell, almost crushing Albert to death as he quickly scrambled out of harm's way. A few days later, Albert had a problem with the crank of his car. He somehow hit himself on the head with the crank, and he fell to the ground, unconscious. When Albert awoke, he still couldn't figure out how his head could have been struck by that stupid crank.

After those two lucky breaks, or unlucky breaks, according to which way you look at it, Albert had a third accident. In August 1925, Albert again was working under his car in his indoor garage, with the engine running. Being the good wife, Ruth brought her husband a cool whiskey and soda to help him battle the heat. Ruth also told Albert how proud she was that he was such a great mechanic. Ruth then exited the garage, and a few minutes after Albert drank the whiskey, he began to feel drowsy. Albert glanced at the garage doors, and he was shocked to find that instead of the doors being open, they were now tightly closed, which was causing him to inhale noxious carbon monoxide fumes from the tailpipe of his running car.

Ruth Snyder related these three incidents to Judd Gray. Even if Albert Snyder didn't realize what was happening, Gray sure did.

"What are you trying to do?" Gray asked Ruth. "Kill the poor guy?"

"Momsie can't do it alone," Ruth said. "She needs help. Lover Boy will have to help her."

At the time, Judd Gray thought, since they had been drinking, it was the alcohol talking, not Ruth. But the next time they met, Gray realized for the first time Ruth had been serious about killing her husband.

After a strenuous bout of lovemaking, Ruth blurted out triumphantly, "We'll be okay for money," she said. "I've just tricked Albert into taking out some hefty life insurance. He thinks it's only for $1,000, but it's really for $96,000, if he dies by accident. I put three different policies in front of him and only let him see the space where you sign. I told him it was a thousand buck policy in triplicate. He's covered for $1,000, $5,000, and $45,000, with a double indemnity clause, in case of an accidental death."

Even after Ruth Snyder had told Judd Gray that she was intent on killing her husband for the life insurance settlements, Gray still had his doubts. While the two love birds continued carrying on their torrid affair, Albert Snyder was nearly killed in three more "accidents."

In July 1926, Albert fell asleep on his living room couch and almost died because someone had accidentally left on the gas jets in the kitchen. In January 1927, Albert had a violent case of the hiccups. Ruth said she had the perfect cure for pickups, and she handed her husband a glass of bichloride of mercury. Albert guzzled down the drink, and he immediately became violently ill. Yet, Albert did not die. The very next month Albert Snyder again fell asleep on his living room couch, and he almost expired, because someone had inadvertently left on the gas tap in the living room.

After trying to kill her husband six times, Ruth Snyder knew she needed help if she were to be successful. She told Judd Gray, "My husband has turned into a brute! He's even bought a gun and says he'll shoot me with it!"

In February 1927, Ruth Snyder and Judd Gray were trysting in the Waldorf-Astoria hotel in midtown Manhattan. Ruth was firmly in charge, and after giving Gray a nice roll in the hay, she ordered Gray to go to Kingston, New York, to purchase chloroform, a window sash weight, and picture wire. She told him, that way "we have three means of killing him. One of them must surely work."

Gray protested, but Ruth was not to be deterred. She said, "If you don't do as I say, that's the end of us in bed. You can find yourself another Momsie to sleep with. Only nobody else would have you but me."

Gray whined that he was not the type to commit murder, but Ruth kept on applying the pressure. One night, when Albert and their daughter Lorraine were not at home, Ruth brazenly brought Gray to her Queens Village house. They went upstairs to her daughter's room, and they had passionate sex. Gray at this point, absolutely terrified that he would not be able to enjoy Ruth's mad lovemaking anymore, reluctantly agreed to participate in the murder of Albert Snyder.

From that point on, Ruth did all the planning, and Gray did what she told him to do. They had several clandestine meetings, where

Ruth laid out the step-by-step procedure on how they would kill her husband. One such meeting took place at Henry's Swedish Restaurant, with Ruth's daughter Lorraine sitting at the same table with them, but not truly understanding what they were talking about: that her father was in imminent danger of being murdered.

In the early morning hours of March 20, 1927, Gray, fortified by more than a few sips of whiskey from a pint bottle, boarded a bus from downtown Manhattan to the Snyder house in Queens. The house was empty, because Ruth and Albert Snyder, along with their daughter Lorraine, were at a bridge party at the home of one of their neighbors, a Mrs. Milton Fidgeon. Ruth had left the side door unlocked, allowing Gray to enter the house. Gray hid himself in an empty bedroom upstairs. Gray even brought an Italian newspaper to plant later as a red herring for the police.

At around 2 a.m., the Snyder family returned home. By this time Albert Snyder was quite drunk. He immediately went to bed and fell asleep in an alcohol-induced stupor. Ruth put Lorraine to bed, and then she slipped down the hall to the extra bedroom where Gray was hiding. Ruth was wearing just a slip and a negligee.

She kissed Gray, and then said, "Have you found the sash weight?" Gray told her he had. Ruth said, "Keep quiet then. I'll be back as quickly as I can."

A few minutes later, Ruth left the master bedroom and entered the bedroom where Gray was waiting. They finished the last of the whiskey Gray had brought with him, then she grabbed Gray by the hand and said, "Okay, this is it."

Ruth led Gray to the master bedroom. Gray was wearing rubber gloves so he wouldn't leave any fingerprints. Ruth was carrying the window sash weight, the chloroform, and the piano wire.

When they opened the bedroom door, Gray saw Albert Snyder for the first time. After they closed the bedroom door behind them, Gray raised the sash weight, brought it over his head, and smashed it feebly down on Albert Snyder's head. It was such an inconsequential blow, Albert Snyder sat up in bed and tried to defend himself.

Gray brought the sash down on Albert Snyder's head a second time, this time drawing a little blood. Albert Snyder, now enraged, clutched Gray's necktie and began to strangle him with it.

Gray screamed like a little girl, "Help Momsie! For God's sake, help!"

Ruth grabbed the fallen sash weight, swung it over her head, and with all her considerable might, she smashed it down onto her husband's head. It was a debilitating blow, but Albert Snyder, now semi-conscious, was still alive. With her manlike strength, Ruth Snyder pinned her twitching husband's body down, and she stuffed cotton, laced with chloroform, into his nostrils and into his mouth. As Gray stood dumbfounded, Ruth tied her husband's hands and feet, and then she strangled her husband to death with the piano wire.

With Albert Snyder now quite dead, Ruth and Gray got busy washing the blood from their clothes. Having done so, Gray put on a clean blue shirt that belonged to Albert.

To make it look like a robbery gone awry, Ruth hid all her jewelry and furs, and also the sash that had been one of the murder weapons. Then they went downstairs to the living room and messed up all the pillows and furniture, to make it look like robbers had overturned everything looking for valuables. That done, Gray loosely tied up Ruth, gagged her with cheesecloth, and left her in the empty bedroom with the Italian newspaper next to her.

Gray was scheduled to travel to the Onondaga Hotel in Syracuse, New York to resume selling corsets. But before he left, he looked back at Ruth and said, "It may be two months, it may be a year, and maybe never before you see me again."

Right after dawn, Lorraine Snyder was awakened by a loud tapping sound that seemed to come from the hallway. She called out to both her parents, but she got no reply. Lorraine ran out into the hallway, and she spotted her mother bound and gagged on the floor. Lorraine untied her mother and took the gag out of her mother's mouth.

Ruth jumped to her feet, and she ran from the house screaming, waking her neighbors Harriet and Louis Mulhauser.

Ruth told them, crying, "It was dreadful, just dreadful! I was attacked by a prowler. He tied me up. He must have been after my jewels." Then she paused, "Is Albert all right?"

Louis Mulhauser ran into the Snyder house, up the stairs and into the master bedroom. He found Albert Snyder bound and dead, with two massive head wounds.

The police were called in immediately, and they were soon suspicious about the way the living room had been tossed. The police interrogated Ruth Snyder as if she were the perpetrator of a husband's demise. Nevertheless, Ruth stuck to her outlandish story.

She insisted to the police, "I was attacked by a big, rough-looking guy of about 35 with a black mustache. He was a foreigner, I guess some kind of Eyetalian."

Dr. Harry Hansen was called in by the police to examine Albert Snyder's body and to examine Ruth Snyder for any sign that she had been assaulted. After examining Albert's body, and Ruth too, Dr. Hansen was convinced that Ruth Snyder's story was a complete fabrication. He gave his findings to Police Commissioner George McLaughlin, and the police commissioner agreed with Dr. Hansen's conclusions. McLaughlin immediately sent 60 policemen to surround the Snyder residence, whereby Ruth was immediately arrested for questioning.

While Ruth was being grilled at the station house, the police searched the Snyder residence. They found Ruth's rings and necklaces under a mattress, and a fur coat hanging in a closet. That convinced the police that Ruth had made up the entire episode and was most likely responsible for her husband's death.

The police also found an address book, with the names of 28 different men in it, including the name of Judd Gray. They also found a canceled check made out to Gray by Ruth Snyder for $200. Now the police knew that Ruth Snyder had had an accomplice.

Armed with this information, the police applied the screws to Ruth Snyder. They hoodwinked her into making a loose confession, by telling her that Judd Gray had already been arrested and had named her as the killer of her husband. Ruth, incensed that her lover would rat her out so quickly, finally admitted that she had indeed taken part in the plan to kill her husband, but she pinned everything on the shy corset salesman.

"But I didn't aim a single blow on Albert," Ruth told the police. "That was all Judd's doing. At the last moment, I tried to stop him, but it was too late!"

Realizing she had been tricked, Ruth Snyder then told police where they could find Judd Gray. The police cornered Gray in a Syracuse hotel and arrested him. Immediately, the usually quiet Gray began talking nonstop. He admitted everything, exactly as it happened, naming Ruth Snyder as the instigator of the whole sordid affair.

"I would have never killed Snyder, but for her," Gray said. "She had this power over me. She just told me what to do, and I did it."

The New York City newspapers played up the trial as "The Granite Woman," versus the "Man of Putty." The trial, which started on April 18, 1927, lasted 18 days. During the trial, Ruth Snyder was dressed entirely in black (obviously in mourning for her dearly-departed husband). She wore a crucifix on a chain around her neck, and she continuously fiddled with rosary beads which were clutched in both hands on her lap. Judd Gray, dressed in a double-breasted, blue pinstriped suit, with fastidiously pressed trousers, sat impassively, as if he was resigned to his fate.

Celebrities from around the country attended the trial, with the thought of writing books and possibly making movies about the murder. Those people included mystery writer Mary Roberts Rinehart, director D. W. Griffith, author Will Durant, actress Nora Bayes, and evangelists Billy Sunday and Aimee Semple McPherson.

One of the New York City's top crime reporters, Peggy Hopkins Joyce, wrote in the *New York Daily Mirror*. "Poor Judd Gray! He hasn't IT! He hasn't anything. He's just a sap who kissed and was told on. This 'Putty Man' was wonderful modeling material for the Swedish-Norwegian vampire. She was passionate, and she was cold-blooded. Her passion was for Gray; her cold-bloodedness was for her husband. You know women can do things to men that make men crazy. I mean, they can exert their influence over them in such a way that men will do almost anything for them. And I guess that is what Ruth did to Judd."

The trial itself was a three-ring circus, in which each defendant blamed the other for the murder of Albert Snyder. Ruth Snyder said on the witness stand that it was Judd Gray who had dragged her to illegal speakeasies and nightclubs. And it was he who drank until he got drunk. Ruth said she didn't drink herself, and certainly never smoked.

Then she told the Big Lie.

Ruth said under oath that it was Judd Gray who had insisted that she take out an expensive life insurance policy on husband's life.

Ruth told the court, "Once, he even sent me poison and told me to give it to my husband."

When Judd Gray took the stand, he was a much more believable witness than Ruth Snyder had been. Gray told the court that Ruth Snyder had tried to kill her husband several times previously, but had been unsuccessful every time.

Gray said under oath, "I told her she was crazy, when she told me that she had given her husband poison as a cure for hiccups. I said to her that it was a hell of a way to cure hiccups."

The entire time Gray was on the witness stand, Ruth Snyder sat with her head bowed, crying incessantly and fingering her rosary beads. Ruth's outbursts of sorrow were so loud, the judge glowered at her and told her to control herself.

With a brilliant summation to the jury, Gray's attorney tried to save his client from the electric chair.

Gray's attorney told the jury that his client was, "The most tragic story that has ever gripped the human heart." He said Judd Gray was a, "law-abiding citizen who had been duped and dominated by a designing, deadly conscienceless, abnormal woman, a human serpent, a human fiend in a disguise of a woman." Gray's attorney also said that Judd Gray had been "drawn into this hopeless chasm when reason was gone, mind was gone, manhood was gone, and when his mind was weakened by lust and passion."

On May 9, after the jury deliberated only 98 minutes, Ruth Brown Snyder and Judd Gray were both found guilty of first-degree premeditated murder. The judge immediately sentenced both of them to die in the electric chair at Sing Sing prison. As a display of the public irrationality over the sensational case, in her prison cell while she awaited execution, Ruth Snyder received 164 marriage proposals.

On January 12, 1928, Judd Gray sat in the electric chair first. After telling the Warden that he had received a letter from his wife forgiving him, he told the Warden that, "He was ready to go and had nothing to fear."

Four minutes after Gray received the juice, Ruth Snyder sat down and was blindfolded in the electric chair. An enterprising reporter from the *New York Daily News* somehow slipped into the execution room with a tiny camera strapped to his ankle. At the instant the electric shock jolted Ruth Snyder's body, the reporter snapped Ruth Snyder's picture. That death picture appeared on the front page of the *New York Daily News* the following day.

In 1944, the highly successful and critically acclaimed movie *Double Indemnity*, starring Barbara Stanwyck and Fred MacMurray, was released. The plot was based on the Ruth Brown Snyder and

Judd Gray murder case. In 2007, the American Film Institute listed *Double Indemnity* as the 29th best movie on their list of the top 100 American movies of all-time.

Part 2 – Riots:

The Anti-Abolition Riots of 1834

It started as a peaceful service given by a black minister at the Chatham Street Chapel, but it transformed into four days of riots that turned the streets of New York City into a cauldron of hate.

In the early 1800's, there was a vibrant movement in the United States to end slavery. Yet, there was no other place in the country that displayed more animosity towards blacks than the mean streets of Manhattan's Lower East Side. The Abolitionist Movement (to abolish slavery) was spearheaded by men like William Lloyd Garrison, and bothers Arthur and Lewis Tappan. Yet, the hatred for black slaves permeated throughout New York City and was incited by the ruling Irish faction of Tammany Hall. This malevolence was punctuated by a multitude of atrocities, perpetrated against the slaves by the Irish Five Points street gangs, which Tammany Hall overtly protected from prosecution for their heinous crimes.

In 1833, aided by the fiery speeches of William Lloyd Garrison, slavery was abolished throughout the British Empire. Many of the Brits living in America also spoke out vociferously against slavery. This did not go over too well with the powers that be at Tammany Hall, which had convinced the Irish street gangs that the Abolitionists were looking to transform America back into a British colony.

Anti-Abolitionist James Watson Webb provoked the Irish gangs even further, when he printed in his *Courier and Enquirer* that, "Abolitionists had told their daughters to marry blacks, black dandies in search of white wives were promenading Broadway on horseback, and Arthur Tappan had divorced his wife and married a negress."

All Webb's statements were lies, but they were believed by the rabble nevertheless.

On July 7, 1834, a group of black slaves gathered in the Chatham Street Chapel to hear a sermon by a black minister. In the audience, lending his support, was Arthur Tappan. The sermon had just begun, when members of the New York Sacred Music Society broke in, claiming they had rented the chapel for the evening. The slaves, who had already paid for the use of the chapel, refused to leave. The street gangs, with members of the Plug Uglies, Forty Thieves, and Roach Guards, banded together and attacked the slaves with leaded canes, seriously injuring several slaves.

An angry mob had formed outside the chapel, and as the police arrived to try to quell the disturbance, Tappan hurried from the scene to his house on Rose Street, which is now the site of the New York City Municipal Building. Knowing he was an avowed abolitionist, a crowd followed Tappan, and as he rushed inside, they pelted his home with rocks.

Webb's paper predictably lied again, when he described the event as a "Negro riot," owing to "Arthur Tappan's mad impertinence." *The Commercial Advertiser*, another pro-slavery rag, said, "Gangs of blacks were preparing to set the city ablaze."

This was just the beginning of a string of atrocities. The next night, a mob of gang members broke down the door of the Chatham Street Chapel. And while they held an impromptu meeting inside, W.W. Wilder yelled, "To the Bowery Theater!"

The reason for their attack on the Bowery Theater was because its manager, and British actor, George P. Farren, another avowed abolitionist, had recently said of the pro-slavery crowd, "Damn the Yankees; they are a damn set of jackasses, and fit to be gulled."

Farren had also just fired an American actor, and as a result, anti-abolitionists posted handbills, detailing Farren's actions, throughout New York City.

An estimated 4000 rioters broke down the doors of the Bowery Theater, interrupting the performance of beloved American actor Edwin Forrest, who was a favorite of the Five Point gangs. Forrest tried to quiet the angry mob, but they insisted on knowing the whereabouts of Farren, who was hiding somewhere on the premises. Before the mob could take the place apart looking for Farren, with the intention of hanging him, a large contingent of police officers arrived and drove the mob from the theater with billy clubs.

Still, the mob was not through. They yelled, "To Arthur Tappan's house!"

Tappan and his family had already escaped before the mob showed up. Yet, when the mob did arrive, they tore down Tappan's house, board by board. They also piled Tappan's furniture into the street, and set it on fire until there was nothing left but a painting of George Washington.

As one rioter tried to throw the Washington painting into the fire, another one ripped it from his hands saying, "It's George Washington! For God's sake, don't burn Washington!"

The mob rampaged through the city, torturing and raping black slaves and even gouging out the eyes of an Englishman, after they had ripped off his ears. The worst rioting was in the Five Points area, where dozens of houses, including St. Phillip's Church, were burned to the ground. Several English sailors and black slaves were captured and mutilated. Word soon spread in the streets that every house in the Five Points area that did not have a candle burning in its window would be burned down. In minutes, candles appeared in every window; saving the neighborhood from destruction at the hands of the out-of-control racist lunatics.

On the afternoon of July 11, Mayor Cornelius Lawrence issued a proclamation asking all good citizens to band together to stop the rioting. He also ordered Major General Shadford to call in the 27th Regiment of the National Guard Infantry. At 9 p.m., around 300 Five Point Gang members assembled before the Laight Street Church, which was run by vocal abolitionist Reverend Samuel Hanson Cox. The church was guarded by several New York City policemen, but the mob charged anyway, forcing the outmanned policemen to run for their lives.

As the mob destroyed the church, Mayor Lawrence ordered the infantry into action. Armed with clubs, bayonets, muskets, and pistols, the infantry drove the rioters from several downtown churches, and the surrounding streets, back into the Five Points area.

The next day, armed soldiers and policemen scoured the Five Points, looking for known mob members. They rounded up and arrested 150 Five Pointers, but then, inexplicably, Tammany Hall stepped in and released almost all of them.

Only 20 gang members, out of the thousands who pillaged the streets of New York City in July of 1834, were ever tried, convicted, and sent to jail.

The Flour Riots of 1837

The flour problem began with the 1835 Great New York City Fire, which destroyed almost 700 downtown buildings. Nearly the entire New York City financial center, including the city's lifeblood - the banks - was burned to the ground. Unable to obtain loans, owners of factories and other downtown businesses, were not able to rebuild, putting tens of thousands of New Yorkers out of work.

By 1837, New York City had sunk into the depths of a recession. With no jobs and no money, people's diets sometimes consisted of little more than simple buttered or jammed bread. The poor of the city began to panic, when they discovered that flour, needed to make their daily bread, would become so expensive they would not be able to afford to buy it.

Matters were made worse, when reports from Virginia and other wheat producing states said there was a scarcity of wheat, from which flour was made, and a rise in price was inevitable. At the beginning of January 1837, wheat started at $5.62 cents a barrel. Within days, it had risen to $7 a barrel; then to $12 a barrel. There were rumors that in a few weeks, wheat would go to an incredible $20 a barrel.

The hardest hit were the poor people, who lived in the slums of the Five Points, Bowery, and the Fourth Ward areas on the Lower East Side of Manhattan. Besides the increase in the price of wheat, meat prices had doubled and coal to heat their hovels rose to $10 a ton. People became desperate, and poor souls who were not normally crooks felt they had no choice but to commit petty crimes in order to put food on their family's table.

On February 1, 1837, news circulated that New York City had only four weeks supply of flour left and that the large flour and grain depot in Troy, New York, contained only 4,000 barrels of flour, rather than the usual 30,000 barrels. The newspapers began sensationalizing the issue, when they stated in their editorials that certain merchants were hoarding wheat and flour in anticipation of the rising prices.

The Tammany Hall politicians were adept at causing unrest between the poor Irish, who populated the slums of Lower Manhattan, and anyone with either money or prestige. Never letting a crisis go to waste, Tammany Hall began spreading unfounded rumors that England was refusing to send flour to the United States. The message was compounded by the untruth that the Old Mother Country's intention was to starve the poor Irish in America, as a repayment for the rancor between Ireland and England which had existed for centuries.

On February 10, 1837, a crowd of nearly 6,000 slum-dwellers, from the Five Points, Fourth Ward, and Bowery areas, met at City Hall Park. Running the meeting from atop the steps of City Hall were Tammany Hall titans like Moses Johnson, Paul Hedle, Warden Hayward, and Alexander Ming Jr. There it was decided that two businesses in particular - Hart and Company on Washington Street, and SH. Herrick & Company on Coenties Slip - were packed with both flour and wheat, and were holding back distribution, hoping for future monetary gain when the prices rose.

One of the speakers said, "Fellow citizens, Mr. Eli Hart has 53,000 barrels of flour in his store. Let us go there and offer him $8 a barrel, and if he does not take it......"

The speaker stopped in mid-sentence, but his implication was clear.

When the talking was over, the crowd stampeded from City Hall Park, and they headed down Broadway, west on Cortland and onto Washington Street. When the watchmen protecting Hart's Store saw the surging mob, they quickly ran inside, and they locked the three huge iron doors. But they forgot to insert the inside bar on the center door.

Eli Hart was viewing the mob unrest from a safe distance, and he immediately ran to City Hall, asking for police protection. Twenty policemen rushed to the scene, but they were beaten back by the rioters and their clubs taken away from them. The newly elected mayor of New York City, Aaron Clark, hurried up the steps of the store, and he tried to quell the angry mob. However, after he was showered with stones and bricks, Clark was forced to run for this life.

The rioters then rushed into the building and wrenched one of the iron doors from its hinges. Using it as a battering ram, they bashed down the other two iron doors, then they busted inside. Once inside, the mob entered the storerooms, then rolled approximately 1,000 bushels of wheat and 500 barrels of flour into the street. They smashed the bushels and barrels, until thousands of rioters were knee deep in the flour and wheat.

People started to sing, "Here goes flour at eight dollars a barrel!"

Women filled their apron and skirts with flour, while men used their hats and pockets to pilfer the goods. Even young children got into the act, scooping up what they could carry on their frail bodies.

Suddenly, the 27th Regiment of the National Guard arrived, and they confronted the rioters. Using bayonets and clubs, the National Guard stabbed and clubbed as many rioters as they could lay their hands on. Eventually, they captured scores of the worst offenders, and they started marching them to the Tombs Prison. However, before they got very far, more rioters attacked the National Guard, and they rescued dozens of prisoners, and in the process, tore the police commissioner's coat right off his back. Forty rioters were finally hustled to the Tombs, where they were tried and convicted, and sent to Sing Sing Prison.

While the rioters carted off their dead and wounded from in front of Hart's store, another contingent headed to the store of S.H. Herrick & Company. There the mob smashed the doors and windows with stones and bats, and within ten minutes, they were able to destroy an additional 30 barrels of flour and 100 bushels of wheat.

Then, without any apparent reason, the mob suddenly disbursed and headed back to their slums, their thirst for destruction finally sated.

The very next day, the price of flour increased one dollar.

Astor Place Theater Riots of 1849

One of the worst riots in New York City history took place on May 10, 1849. It started over an impassioned disagreement over who had the better Shakespearian Actor: the United States, or hated Mother England.

British actor William Macready was considered to be the most accomplished actor on both sides of the pond. Yet Macready, who called himself an aristocrat, was a snob, who looked down on America in general and their inferior actors in particular. One of those actors who caused Macready to sniff in superiority was the Philadelphia-born Edwin Forrest, a self-taught thespian, who was the darling of the rough and tumble New York City crowd. To make matters worse for Forrest and his followers, the New York City aristocracy much preferred the foreigner Macready instead of the homegrown Forrest.

In 1848, Forrest, on a mission to prove to the world that he was the equal of any actor alive, traveled to London, England, to play Hamlet. Even though Forrest dined with Macready the night before Forrest's performance, when Forrest took the stage he was brutally hissed by the audience. Forrest's performance was panned viciously in the London newspapers and repeated in the American press. Forrest blamed this on Macready, and by the time Forrest arrived back in the United States, there was a global feud ready to explode.

Two New Yorkers were instrumental in fanning the flames of discontent concerning the rude treatment of their homeboy Forrest in England. One was Captain Isaiah Rynders, who owned the notorious Empire Club on Park Row. Rynders was also the mob boss, who controlled all the vicious gangs in the Five Points area. The other instigator was E. Z. C. Judson, who wrote under the pen name - Ned Buntline. Both men hated the English, and in the weekly newspaper, *Ned Buntline's Own*, Buntline turned a mere heated actors' dispute into an international incident.

The tension mounted, when it was announced in the New York City press that Macready would make a four-week "farewell" appearance in America, commencing on May 7, 1849. His first show was scheduled to be at the new Astor Place Theater, on Astor Place in Manhattan. As soon as Macready graced the stage with his presence, Rynders rose from his seat, and in concert with hundreds of his gang thugs in attendance, they peppered Macready with rotten eggs, ripe tomatoes, and old shoes. Macready, incredulous at the blatant disrespect for his great talents, thundered off the stage. He canceled the rest of his four-week engagement and vowed never to appear in the United States again.

This caused great consternation among the blue-bloods in New York City's society crowd. Quickly, they assembled a petition with 47 signatures, which included those of Washington Irving and Herman Melville, begging Macready to stay and continue his tour. Macready, against his better judgment, caved in and agreed to give it one more try.

The news hit the newspapers, that on May 10, just three days after he was rudely chased from the stage, Macready would appear as Macbeth in *Macbeth*; again at the Astor Place Theater. Coincidentally, Forrest also opened that same night, playing Spartacus in *The Gladiator*, in a playhouse a mile south of the Astor Place Theater. The newspapers played up the rivalry and the British crew of a docked Cunard liner said they would make their presence known at Macready's performance, lest an unruly American mob again tried to insult their countryman.

This incited Captain Rynders to plaster New York City with thousands of posters saying, "*Workingmen, shall Americans or English rule this city? The crew of the English steamer has threatened all Americans who shall dare to express their opinion this night at the English Aristocratic Opera House! We advocated no violence, but free expression of opinion is to all men!*"

New York City mayor Caleb C. Woodhull anticipated a riot, and he sent 350 policemen, under the command of Police Chief G.W. Matsell, to the Astor Place Theater to quell any possible disturbances. In addition, General Sanders, of the New York Militia, assembled eight companies of guardsmen and two troops of Calvary to patrol the area around the playhouse.

When the show started, all 1,800 seats had been sold, with the pro-Macready crowd vastly outnumbering the pro-Forrest crowd. It was estimated that more than 20,000 people stood outside the theater, making Astor Place, from Broadway to the Bowery, one large sea of discontent.

At 7:40 p.m., the play started, and the first two scenes played out without any interruption. However, when Macready majestically strode on stage for the third scene, all hell broke loose. Captain Rynders and his gangs hooted and hollered and hissed at Macready. Outside, the angry crowd, hearing the animosity inside, started to bum-rush the theater. They threw rocks and stones, breaking all the theater's windows. And just because they could, the mob smashed all the street lamps in the area too.

The police attacked the angry mob with clubs, but to no avail. The mob screamed "Burn the damned den of aristocracy."

The police were getting the worst of the riot, and at 9 p.m., the first of the militia arrived. They too were pelted by bricks and stones. Ned Buntline was at the head of the angry mob chanting, "Workingmen! Shall Americans or Englishmen rule? Shall the sons whose fathers drove the baseborn miscreants from these shores give up liberty?"

Chief Matsell, after being hit with a 20-pound rock in the chest, gave the order for the militia to shoot into the crowd. And they did just that, hitting men, women, and children, and even a lady who was sleeping in her bed 150 yards from the theater.

When the dust cleared hours later, 22 people were killed and 150 were injured. Five of those who were injured, died within five days. 86 rioters were arrested, including Ned Buntline, who received a year in jail and a $250 fine. Captain Rynders escaped without arrest, or injury, only to torment the city for many years to come.

The lawmen were not without their own injuries. More than a hundred policemen and militia were injured by rocks and stones, and another six were shot; but none died.

The next night, another mob tried to burn down the Astor Place Theater. But they were beaten back by a new battalion of militia, which had been brought into the city in case of further disturbances.

On the night of May 12, another crowd assembled at the New York Hotel, where Macready was staying, screaming for him to come out and be hanged like a man. However, Macready somehow slipped away. He boarded a train to New Rochelle, and then to Boston. From Boston, he sailed to England, never again to set foot in America.

The Civil War Draft Riots of 1863

Never in the history of New York has there been a more brutal mass insurrection than the New York City Civil War Draft Riots of 1863.

In March of 1863, the seeds were planted for these riots when President Abraham Lincoln issued a proclamation, called The Conscription Act (or Enrollment Act), stating he needed 300,000 more men to be drafted into the Northern Army, to beat back the Southern Rebels in the Civil War. This act required every male citizen, between the ages of 20 and 40, to be drafted into the war. Each man who joined the army was given a bounty of up to $500, as an enlistment bonus. The gravest inequity, however, was that for the sum of $300 a man could buy himself out of being drafted. The rich could afford the $300, but the poor could not, which led to the Civil War being called "A rich man's war and a poor man's fight."

New York City (only Manhattan at the time) had more than 800,000 citizens, of which more than half were foreign. Of that half, half again were poor Irish, who had no desire to fight in a war to end the slavery of Negroes, whom they despised. These poor, low-class Irish people had settled in the Five Points and in the Mulberry Bend areas in downtown Manhattan (the 6th Ward), and also in the 4th Ward near the East River. In these slums, gangs like the Plug Uglies, the Bowery Boys, the Roach Guards, and the Dead Rabbits, committed atrocious crimes. And this downtown area is where the draft rioters began their bloodthirsty march.

President Lincoln had announced that Draft Day in New York City would commence on Saturday, July 11. On that day, with only minor disturbances throughout the city, 1,236 men were drafted into the war. When the draft ended that day, it was announced that the draft would bypass Sunday and continue again on Monday morning.

However, the seeds of discontent grew during the rest of the weekend, spurred by an article in Saturday evening's *Leslie's Illustrated*, which stated, "It came like a thunderclap on the people, as men read their names in the fatal list, the feeling of indignation and resistance soon found vent in words, and a spirit of resistance spread fast and far. The number of poor men exceeded that of the rich, their number to draw from being that much greater, but this was viewed as proof of the dishonesty in the whole proceeding."

As Monday morning drew near, the poor slum-living Irish began planning how to voice their displeasure, and it wouldn't be pleasant. At 6 a.m. Monday, men and women started spilling out of the downtown slums, and they began their resolute march to the north. At every street corner, more discontents joined their forces, and the group became so huge it split into two groups. It was estimated that eventually 50,000 to 70,000 people took part in the four-day Draft Riots, and the New York City Metropolitan Police had only 3,000 men to combat the rioters.

As the rioters moved north along Fifth and Sixth Avenues, they turned east and made a beeline toward the main draft office, at 46th Street and Third Avenue. Police Superintendent John A. Kennedy, realizing trouble was brewing, dispatched 60 police officers to guard the Third Avenue Draft Office, and another 69 to guard the draft office at Broadway and 29th Street.

The rioters on Third Avenue were led by the volunteer firemen attached to Engine Company 33, known as The Black Joke. They consisted of members of the Plug Uglies street gang, who by now had stopped traffic completely and were pulling people out of their carts. Signs in the crowd were held saying "NO DRAFT!!", when suddenly someone in the crowd shot a pistol up into the air, and the riots commenced.

The mob threw bricks and stones at the draft office, breaking all the windows in the building. Then they surged forward, thousands of them, while 60 cops tried in vain to hold them back. The rioters stepped over the now-battered and unconscious policemen, and as draft officials jumped out the rear windows of the building, the mob set fire to the Third Avenue Draft Office.

Meanwhile, Superintendent Kennedy had left Police Headquarters at 300 Mulberry Street, wearing civilian clothes as a disguise. He took a horse carriage to 46th Street and Lexington Avenue, but when he saw the smoke, he jumped out of the carriage and proceeded on foot.

Kennedy was immediately recognized, and beaten to a bloody pulp, until he was unconscious. A Good Samaritan named John Egan saved Kennedy, when he announced to the mob that Kennedy was dead. Kennedy was covered with a gunny sack and put into a wagon, which drove him to Police Headquarters. When he was examined by doctors, Kennedy was found to have 72 bruises on his body and over two dozen cuts.

The rioters then attacked the Colored Orphans Asylum, on Fifth Avenue and 46th Street. As the rioters stormed the building, 50 matrons and attendants snuck 200 Negro children out a secret back exit. The mob rushed in, stole blankets, toys, and bedding, and then set fire to the building. One young Negro girl, who was accidentally left behind, was found hiding under a bed. She was dragged out and savagely beaten to death.

All throughout the streets of New York City, angry Irish mobs chased Negroes, whom they blamed for the drafts in the first place. The Negroes who were caught, were beaten to death and sometimes hanged. As their bodies hung from trees and rafters, mad Irish woman, glee in their eyes, stabbed the dead Negroes' bodies, while they danced under lit torches, and sang obscene songs.

Finally, Mayor George Updyke wired the War Department in Washington D.C. for help. During the next three days of unspeakable mayhem, hundreds of buildings were burned down, innumerable business looted, and Negroes were killed for no other reason than for the color of their skin. When the order was given, the United States Militia, armed, trained, and 10,000 strong, stormed New York City to quell the riots.

On Tuesday, July 14, New York Governor Horatio Seymour stood on the steps of City Hall, and said to the assembled crowd "I have received a dispatch from Washington that the draft is now suspended."

Governor Seymour was booed and jeered, and the riots continued for two more days.

It is impossible to estimate how many people were killed in the four-day riots. The New York Post reported that, under the blanket of darkness, the bodies of dead rioters were shipped across the East River, and quietly buried in Brooklyn. Police Superintendent Kennedy put the total dead at 1,155, but that did not include those buried secretly at night. Of the tens of thousands of rioters involved, and despite the brutal murders of scores of Negroes, only 19 people were tried and convicted of any crimes. The average prison sentence was a mere five years.

Diarist George Templeton Strong summed up the disgrace of the 1863 New York City Civil War Draft Riots, when he wrote "This is a nice town to call itself a center of civilization."

The Great Rocking Chair Scandal Riots of 1901

Nothing incites the general public more than someone trying to charge for something that previously cost nothing. Yet, that's exactly what entrepreneur Oscar F. Spate tried to do in the New York City public parks in the blistering summer of 1901.

It all started in Central Park on June 22, 1901, when a group of people spotted rows of bright green rocking chairs along the park mall near the casino. Usually in this same spot stood rows of uncomfortable, hard, wooden benches, so it was a pleasure indeed for the park-goers to sit and rock and enjoy the wondrous summer day.

Suddenly, two broad-shouldered men approached the rocking-chair sitters. They wore identical gray suits, and they carried black satchels with straps over their shoulders. The men in gray told the sitters that these private chairs were for rent, and that if they wanted to continue sitting they had to fork over five cents a day for the better seats and three cents a day for seats not in as preferential a position in the park.

Some people vacated their seats, but others paid. People who did neither were physically ejected from the seats.

When they asked why, the men in gray said, "Them's Mr. Spate's chairs."

This new phenomenon was covered extensively and contentiously in the following day's New York City daily newspapers. And the man on the hot seat was the president of the Park Commission – one George C. Clausen.

It seemed that a few days earlier, Clausen had been visited in his official Park Commission office by a man named Oscar F. Spate. Spate seemed amiable enough, and he offered Clausen a proposition Clausen saw no difficulty in accepting. It seemed that Spate said he wanted to place comfortable rocking chairs in the parks throughout New York City. And for the privilege of doing so, Spate offered the city the tidy sum of $500 a year.

"They do this in London and Paris," Spate told Clausen. "And it would undoubtedly be good for New York City, too."

Clausen agreed with Spate's line of thinking, so he readily

accepted Spate's offer; albeit without first consulting with the other members of the Park Commission. As a result, Clausen graced Spate with a five-year contract, allowing Spate to place his rocking chairs in all the New York City public parks.

With the ink still not dry on his contract, Spate immediately ordered 6,000 chairs, costing around $1.50 each. If Spate's projections were correct, these chairs would earn him an estimated $250-$300 a day.

An associate of Spate's, who asked a newspaper reporter for anonymity, said that Spate had already invested $30,000 in his new venture. The reporter did the math, and he figured the rocking chairs only cost Spate around $9,500, total. Pray tell, where did the other $20,500 go?

Spate's spokesman said nothing that enlightened the reporter.

"Well, there's always expenses in things like this, you know," he told the scribe.

The New York City press knew a story when it hit them in the face, so they managed to track down Spate in his offices in the St. James Building on Broadway and 26th Street near Madison Square Park.

When questioned by the reporters, Spate became indignant.

"I'll put in as many chairs as they will allow," Spate told the reporters. "The attendants who ect the charges are in my pay. They will wear gray uniforms, and each will look after about 50 chairs, from 10 a.m. to 10 p.m. A five-cent ticket entitles the holder to sit in either a five-cent, or a three-cent chair, in any park at any time during that day. But the holder of a three-cent chair can only sit in a three-cent chair."

Spate also told reporters he was doing the city a favor, since charging for the chairs would keep the undesirables (read - the poor) out of the parks, thereby keeping the parks sparkling clean and free of loiterers who leave a mess in their wake.

The outrage from the New York City press and from philanthropists came swiftly. Randolph Guggenheimer, the president of the Municipal Council, said he "saw no good reason for allowing private parties to occupy park grounds and make money through a scheme like this." The New York City Central Federated Union sent a statement to the press denouncing both Spate and Clausen for their "hideous actions." The *New York Tribune* wrote in an editorial,

"This is only another instance of the hopeless stupidity of the present Park Commission." The *New York Journal* also wrote an editorial defending the "rights of poor people to sit in a public park." However, the *New York Times* saw no problem with what Spate was doing, as long as "the prices were regulated properly."

Park Commissioner Clausen tried to defend his actions by telling the press there were always plenty of free benches for people to sit on, except, of course, on Saturdays, Sundays, and holidays. The *New York Tribune* pointed out that those were the days with the biggest demand for seats in the parks.

As this issue became monumental, Spate became more resolute. He ordered that additional chairs be placed in Central Park and also in Madison Square Park, which was across the street from his office. Some people paid to sit, and those who didn't pay were unceremoniously thrown out of the chairs by Spate's thugs in gray suits.

Things quieted down for a few days, as few people protested paying for the seats.

That changed drastically on Wednesday, June 26, 1901, when the city's outside temperature rose above 90 degrees. By Saturday the temperature had risen to 94 degrees and 19 people had perished in New York City due to the insufferable conditions. The temperature reached 97 degrees on Sunday, making it the hottest day on record with the Weather Bureau since June of 1871. On Sunday, 15 more people died, and on Tuesday, with the temperature rising to 99 degrees, 200 deaths were reported. There were 317 heat-related deaths on Wednesday, which made, in the time period from June 28 to July 4, a total of 382 heat-related deaths in Manhattan alone, along with 521 hospitalizations for heat prostration. Altogether, in a seven-day period in the metropolitan district of New York City, which includes Manhattan, Brooklyn, the Bronx, Queens, and Richmond County, there were 797 deaths and 891 heat prostrations.

Things were so bad, that on July 2, the city's hospital ambulance drivers worked 24 hours straight with no time off.

With the city in a heat-related frenzy, harried people hurried to the city's parks, which were now ordered by the Park Commission to stay open all night. When people arrived at the parks, they discovered that many of the free benches were no longer there, and the ones that were still present in the parks had been moved into the sun, making them too hot to sit on.

However, Spate's green chairs were sitting nicely in the shade, making them more attractive to the people fighting the stifling heat.

On Saturday, July 6, the situation reached a boiling point.

A man sat in one of Spate's chairs in Madison Square Park, and he absolutely refused to pay the five cents that Spate's man, Thomas Tully, demanded. Finally, Tully pulled the chair out from under the man, and bedlam ensued.

An angry crowd surrounded Tully and began shouting, "Lynch him! He's Spate's man!"

Tully fought his way through the crowd and sped across the street to the Fifth Avenue Hotel, where he rushed upstairs and locked himself in a room. A crowd had gathered in the hotel lobby for about 30 minutes, when policemen arrived and escorted Tully from the hotel to wherever he called home.

Later that day, with the heat still beating down on the park-goers, another one of Spate's men evicted a boy who was sitting in one of Spate's chairs in Madison Square Park and had refused to pay the required five cents. An angry crowd attacked Spate's man, and when a policeman tried to intervene, he was dumped into the park's fountain. Spate's man fled the park in fear, and after he did, delighted people began taking turns sitting in Spate's chairs (without paying, of course). When nightfall arrived, several people carried Spate's chairs home with them as trophies to grace their own living rooms.

The following day, Sunday, July 7, the uneasiness moved to Central Park, where a huge crowd gathered in defiance of Spate and his green rocking chairs. While two of Spate's men guarded Spate's precious chairs, the crowd marched perilously close to the chairs, chanting to the tune of *Sweet Annie Moore*:

We pay no more!
We pay no more!
No more we pay for park
Chairs anymore!
Clausen made a break
One summer's day.
And now he ain't
Commissioner no more!

As the crowd converged on the chairs, people, who had already paid for the right to sit, abandoned the chairs and fled from the park. One of Spate's men quit his job on the spot, and he also fled the park. However, another one of Spate's men continued to try to collect the chair fees. But he quit, too, after an angry old lady jabbed him in the back of the neck with a hairpin.

On Monday, July 8, Madison Square Park was the site of almost constant rioting. A dozen or so boys went from chair to chair, sitting for as long as they pleased, accompanied by an unruly crowd threatening to hang any of Spate's men who tried to collect any fees.

A brave and foolhardy Spate employee named Otto Berman slapped one boy in the face. The crowd surrounded Berman, and his life was saved by six policemen who bum-rushed Berman out of the park and into safety. Things had gotten so-out-of-control in Madison Square Park, police reinforcements were called in from the nearby West 30th Street police station.

In the late afternoon, two men occupied two of Spate's chairs and offered a thousand dollars to any of Spate's men who could evict them from the chairs.

Two of Spate's men jumped in and tried to collect the reward, but they were promptly beaten to a pulp by the two men, who turned out to the featherweight champion of the world Terry McGovern, and former fighter and then-boxing ring announcer Joe Humphreys.

The police stormed the park and arrested six rioters, whom they led in cuffs to the Thirtieth Street police station. The policemen and the arrestees were followed by a crowd estimated at 200 people, who were marching in lockstep and chanting:

Spate! Spate!
Clausen and Spate!
Spate! Spate!
Clausen and Spate!

On Tuesday, July 9, the riots continued at both Madison Square Park and Central Park. However, the New York City police took a different tactic, when they were ordered by Police Commissioner Michael Murphy not to aid any of Spate's men trying to collect fees and not to arrest any of the rioters, unless court magistrates issued arrest warrants for the individual rioters. At this point, several of the magistrates told the press they would not issue any warrants, which gave the rioters the (wink-wink) go-ahead to do as they pleased with Spate's chairs.

By this time, the president of the Park Commission, George C. Clausen, was figuratively tearing the hair out of his own head. Having first said he could do nothing about the situation without the permission of the rest of the Park Commission, Clausen then reversed himself and said, since he was the one who had confirmed Spate's contract, he could also revoke Spate's contract with New York City. Spate quickly answered by getting a court injunction "restraining Mr. Clausen and the Park Commission from interfering with his valid contract with the City of New York."

In an act of desperation, Spate ordered his men not to place his chairs on the ground, but to pile them in heaps in Madison Square Park and Central Park, and rent them only if they were paid for in advance. However, as soon as someone rented one of Spate's chairs, members of the crowd grabbed the chair and broke it into little pieces.

Soon, the crowd, tired of Spate and his chairs, began bombarding Spate's men with rocks and stones. To avoid serious injury, Spate's men hid behind and under the chairs piled up in heaps. Spate entered both parks himself to try to enforce his contract, but was forced to flee both times; with rocks and stones flying past his head.

Finally, on July 11, a hero named Max Radt, the vice-president of the Jefferson State Bank, went into state Supreme Court and got an injunction forbidding Spate and the Park Commission from charging people to sit in Spate's green rocking chairs. Spate, realizing he was a beaten man, promptly put all his chairs in storage. A few days later, Spate announced to the press he was "abandoning his project."

Oscar F. Spate dropped out of sight and was never seen or heard from again in New York City.

A few weeks later, the Parks Commission issued a press release to the New York City newspapers announcing that the president of the Park Commission, George C. Clausen, had used his own personal money to purchase what was left of Spate's green rocking chairs. These chairs were to be placed in public parks throughout

New York City.

On each of these chairs was stenciled the lettering, "For the Exclusive Use of Women and Children."

And right above the declaration, in large letters, was painted the word "FREE."

Part 3 – Disasters:

Great New York City Fire of 1835

It was the worst fire in New York City's history. But that didn't stop the poor Irish, living in the slums of the Five Points, from going on a dazzling display of looting, which led to one of the biggest free champagne parties in the history of America.

The city was in the throes of one of the coldest winters on record. On the days preceding "The Great Fire," the temperature had dropped as low as 17 degrees below zero. By the night of December 16, 1835, there was two feet of frozen snow on the ground and the temperature was exactly zero frigid degrees. It was so cold, both the Hudson River and East Rivers had completely frozen.

Around 9 p.m., a watchman (the precursor to a New York City policeman) named Warren Hayes was crossing the corner of Merchant (now Beaver Street) and Pearl Street, when he thought he smelled smoke. Hayes looked up at the last floor of a five-story building at 25 Merchant Street, rented by Comstock and Andrews, a famous dry-goods store, and he spotted smoke coming out of a window. Unbeknownst to Hayes, a gas pipe had ruptured and had ignited some coals left on a stove.

Hayes immediately ran through the streets yelling "Fire!!" In minutes, the great fire bell that stood above City Hall began peeling loudly, summoning what was left of the New York City Fire Department. The bell at the Tombs Prison, about a mile north, also started ringing, summoning the volunteer firemen in that area.

In 1832, New York City was stricken with the worst case of cholera in the city's history. Four thousand people died, and more than half of the city's quarter million population fled the city in fear. This decimated the New York City Fire Department, and by 1835, the Fire Department had less than half of its previous members.

The volunteer fire department that responded on December 16, 1835, had spent the previous night fighting a fire on Burlington Street, on the East River, and they were now near exhaustion. By the time the local fire department arrived 30 minutes later, due to 40 mile-a-hour winds, the fire had already spread to 50 structures.

Buildings were going up in flames on Water Street, Exchange Place, Beaver, Front, and South Streets. By midnight, the fire had also consumed Broad and Wall Street, which was the heart of the business and financial center of New York City, if not the entire country. Most of the city's newspaper plants, retail and wholesale stores, and warehouses, were also engulfed by the conflagration.

The call went out to every fire department in the city, but it was of no use. 75 hook and ladder companies were at the scene less than two hours after the fire had started. Hundreds of citizens pitched in, carrying water in buckets, pails, and even tubs. Unfortunately, because of the cold weather, the fire hoses were mostly useless.

In addition, the entire city's cisterns, wells, and fire hydrants were frozen too. Whatever water did stream thinly from the hydrants through the hoses, only went 30 feet into the air, then quickly turned into ice. What made matters worse, due to the high winds, this ice/water mixture, feebly coming out of the hoses, was blown back onto the fireman themselves, and soon scores of firemen were living ice structures. Many firemen poured brandy into their boots to keep their feet from getting frostbite. Some drank the brandy, too, in order to keep the rest of their body warm.

Other firemen raced to the East River, and they started chopping the ice to reach the water below. Black Joke Engine No. 33 was dragged onto the deck of a ship, and it started pumping water through the holes in the ice. Engine No. 33 directed the water though three other engines, until it finally reached the fire on Water Street. However, in just a few hours, those four engines were frozen too and were no longer of any use.

Two buildings were saved in an extremely odd way. Barrels of vinegar were rolled out of the Oyster King Restaurant, in the Downing Building on Garden Street. This vinegar was poured into several fire engines and used to douse the fires in the Downing Building, and in the Journal of Commerce Building next door. However, the vinegar soon ran out and could not be used to save any more structures.

As the city was engulfed in mayhem, a man ran into a church on Garden Street, and he began playing a funeral dirge on an organ, which could be heard all throughout Lower Manhattan. Minutes later, that church caught fire too, and the organist was seen sprinting from the flaming church.

Soon, the fire spread to Hanover Square, Williams Street, Hanover Street, and Exchange Place. Burning cloths and twines from various buildings were blown into the air, and they flew across the East River, igniting the roofs of homes in Brooklyn. The city's blaze was so intense, smoke could be seen as far south as Philadelphia and as far north as New Haven. New York City was so desperate, Philadelphia firemen were summoned from 90 miles away to help fight the blaze.

After consulting with experts, New York City Mayor Cornelius W. Lawrence agreed that the fire could be stopped, if they blew up certain buildings in strategic places, so that the flames could not travel from building to building. The only problem was, the sale of gunpowder was forbidden in New York City. The nearest ample supply was in the Brooklyn Navy Yard, in Red Hook, Brooklyn, as well as on Governors Island.

Mayor Strong sent word that the gunpowder was needed immediately, but it did not arrive until noon on December 17, accompanied by 80 marines and a dozen sailors. The military, with the help of James Hamilton, the son of former Secretary of the Treasury Alexander Hamilton, began blowing up buildings. In a few hours, the blaze was contained at Coenties Slip.

As downtown Manhattan continued smoldering, hundreds of Irish men, women, and children, from the slums of the Five Points area, rushed into the devastated area, eyes sparkling, and hands a-grabbing. For a full 24 hours, the hoodlums looted whatever they could get their hands on: stealing cloaks, frock coats, plug hats, and silk and satin of the finest quality.

Cases and kegs of booze, beer, and wine were smashed open, and the mob drank heartily in the smoky frigid streets. Fights broke out between the drunk and delirious rioters, over who had the right to steal what. Ten thousand bottles of the finest champagne were stolen, too, and what the mob could not guzzle on site, they lugged back to their slums for later consumption.

Noted diarist and future Mayor of New York City, Philip Hone, later wrote, "The miserable wretches, who prowled around the ruins, and became beastly drunk on the champagne and other wines and liquors, with which the streets and roads were lined, seemed to exult in the misfortune of others."

Finally, the area was placed under martial law, and patrolled by the marines from the Navy Yard, and from the Third and Ninth Military Regiments. However, this did not completely stop the looters from continuing their felonious frenzy. Dozens rushed to unaffected areas outside the burn zone, and they torched buildings, so they could loot those buildings too. Five arsonists were arrested by the Marines. But a sixth one, who was caught torching a building on the corner of Stone and Broad, was captured by angry citizens and immediately hung from a tree. His frozen body stood dangling there and was not cut down by the police until three days later.

From the start of the fire, three days had passed until the last spark was extinguished. By then, 17 blocks of lower Manhattan, covering 52 acres and consisting of 693 buildings, had burned to the ground. Two people were killed, and the damages were assessed at $20 million, almost a billion dollars by today's standards.

There was 10 million dollars in insurance money owed for the damages, but only a scant amount of that money was ever paid, since the insurance companies, and the banks, had also burned to the ground, forcing them out of business. Not being able to collect on their insurance, and not being able to get loans from banks that no longer existed, hundreds of businesses that burned to the ground during "The Great New York Fire of 1835" never re-opened.

In 1836, the downtown area was rebuilt, with structures made of stone and concrete, which were less susceptible to spreading fires. Some of those buildings are standing to this day.

The Brooklyn Theater Fire of 1876

It started out as a gala performance of *Two Orphans* at the
Brooklyn Theater on Washington Street in Brooklyn. But thanks to
inefficient and incompetent theater personnel, it wound up being the
third-worst fire, occurring either in a theater or public assembly
building, in the history of the United States of America.

The title roles were played by Maude Harrison and Kate
Claxton, who was thought to be one of the best stage actresses of her
time. Others in the cast included well-known actors Claude
Burroughs, J.B. Studley, H.S. Murdoch, and Mrs. Farren. All would
play leading roles in the tragedy that followed.

The Brooklyn Theater, which seated 1,600 people, was built in
1871. It was an L-shaped brick building with its main entrance on
Washington Street and a secondary entrance on Johnson Street, a
smaller thoroughfare which ran perpendicular to Washington Street
200 feet to the east. One block to the north was what was then
Brooklyn's City Hall. And one block to the south was Fulton Street,
the main thoroughfare to the Manhattan ferries, which brought
theatergoers from the mainland of Manhattan to the Brooklyn
Theater. (The Brooklyn Bridge wasn't built until 1886.)

The Brooklyn Theater had three floors of seating. The ground
floor was called the "Parquet and parquet circle" seating. It
contained 600 seats. The second floor balcony seats were called the
"dress circle" seats, and they seated 550 patrons. The third floor
gallery, which was called the "family circle" seats, contained 450
seats.

The top level family circle seats, at 50 cents a pop, were the
cheapest seats in the house, and it had its own box office on
Washington Street. It also had one set of 7-foot wide stairs, designed
with a zigzag of right-and left-angle turns and leading directly from
the street outside to the third floor. The theater was set up such that
the people in the family circle seats had no access to the balcony
below, or to the main floor of the theater.

This turned out to be their undoing.

The second floor dress circle seats, costing one dollar, had two
flights of stairs to enter and exit the theater. One was a 10-foot wide
set of stairs that led to and from the lobby. The other was a narrower

set of emergency stairs that led to Flood's Alley, a tiny strip of dirt behind the theater. The ground floor door to Flood's Alley was usually locked to stop gatecrashers from entering the theater on the sly.

The ground floor seating was comprised of three price ranges. The least expensive was the parquet seating, disadvantageously situated on the side of the stage and costing 75 cents. The parquet circle seats, which were in the middle of the auditorium, cost $1.50. There were also eight private boxes, four on each side of the stage, which were the most fashionable and expensive seats in the house. Each private box contained six seats. Box seats cost a whopping $10 apiece, a kingly sum in the 1870s.

Illumination in the theater was provided by gas jets in the lobby and in the vestibule. A few gas jets covered by ornamental globes were set on the orchestra floor. Border lights were lined in a row along the proscenium arch, which is the rectangular frame around the stage. These lights had tin on the side facing the audience and were covered by wire netting. Above the boarder lights were thin pieces of cloth that served as scenery. Some of these pieces of cloth dangled precariously close to the boarder lights.

As a precaution, buckets of water were usually kept on the side of the stage in case the dangling scenery caught fire. Plus, there was a fire hose backstage that was connected to a 2 ½-inch water pipe.

On December 5, 1876, approximately a thousand people were in attendance at the Brooklyn Theater. About 400 people were seated in the upper family circle seats (an exact figure was never determined), 360 people sat in the dress circle seats, and 250 people sat in the parquet and parquet circle seats.

Edward B. Dickinson, who was seated in the middle of the parquet seats about five rows from the stage, thought the auditorium floor was not more than half-full. However, Charles Vine, who was sitting in the top family circle seats, thought it was "one of the biggest galleries" he had seen in a long time at the Brooklyn Theater.

Everything was fine until the short intermission between the fourth and fifth acts. During this time, the curtain was down hiding the stage, and the orchestra was playing during the intermission. People in the parquet circle heard loud noises from behind the curtain. But this was not considered unusual.

Seconds before the curtain came down, stage manager, J. W.

Thorpe, saw a small flame coming from the lower part of a drop scenery hanging near the center stage border light. Thorpe later said the flame was about the size of his hand. Thorpe looked for the water buckets, but for some reason they were not where they were supposed to be. He thought about using the fire hose backstage, but so much scenery was in the way, he decided it was quicker to extinguish the fire by beating it with long stage poles. Thorpe directed his carpenters, Hamilton Weaver and William Van Sicken, to attempt to quell the fire by banging it with two large stage poles.

At around 11:20 p.m., the fifth and final act started. When the curtain came down, Kate Claxton, playing a blind orphan girl, was laying on a stack of straw, looking upward. J. B. Studley and H. S. Murdoch had taken their places on stage, in a box set representing an old boathouse on the bank of the Seine. Mary Ann Farren and Claude Burroughs were waiting in the wings for their cues to enter into the scene. Miss Harrison was not in this scene, so she stood backstage and watched the production.

Murdock had delivered just a few lines, when he heard someone whisper "Fire" from backstage. Murdock looked up to the proscenium arch. He saw heavy black smoke and the flickering of small flames. Murdock could see that the fire was spreading quickly upward towards the domed ceiling of the theater. Murdock stopped delivering his lines, but the audience had not yet noticed the fire and smoke.

Murdock heard Claxton whisper, "Go on. They will put it out. Go on."

Murdock finished his lines, and Farren and Burroughs entered the scene from the wings. Miss Claxton had just delivered her lines to Murdock, saying, "I forbid you to touch me. I will beg no more," when flaming parts of the ceiling fell onto the stage, igniting Claxton's costume. Studley hurried over and extinguished the flames on Claxton with his bare hands.

The orchestra, for some reason, broke out into a cheerful song, but it did nothing to quell anyone's fears.

By this time, the people in the theater had realized a fire was occurring, and screams of terror began to reverberate against the theater's walls. Farren and Murdock stopped play acting and stood on one side of the stage, imploring the people to leave quickly and quietly. Claxton and Studley did the same on the other side of the stage.

Claxton yelled to the crowd, who were now on their feet in an extremely agitated state, "You can all go out if you can only keep quiet. We are between you and the flames! Keep cool and walk out quietly!"

But the frenzied crowd had a mind of its own. People ran out into the aisles and panic ensued.

Studley yelled to the crowd, "If I have the presence of mind to stand here between you and the fire, which is right behind me, you ought to have the presence of mind to go out quietly!"

Claxton later told the police, "We were now almost surrounded by flames; it was madness to delay longer. I took Mr. Murdoch by the arm and said 'Come, let us go.' He pulled away from me in a dazed sort of way and rushed into his dressing room, where the fire was even then raging. To leap from the stage into the orchestra, in the hope of getting out through the front of the house, would only add one more person to the frantic struggling mass of human beings, who were trampling each other to death like wild beasts."

Burning timber began raining onto the stage, and the actors were forced to run into the wings. Claxton suddenly remembered there was a small hallway which led from her dressing room, through the basement and into the box office. Claxton ran backstage, met Harrison, and both ladies fled though this passage in their dressing room to the box office outside. On the other hand, Murdock and Burroughs ran back to their dressing rooms to get warmer clothing to fend off the frigid December air outside the theater.

Neither man made it out of the theater alive.

By this time a fire alarm had been sent out from the First Precinct police station, which was next door to the theater. Also, a telegram was sent to Mayor Schroeder, informing him of the dire situation.

Some of the theater's crew ran to the Johnson Street exits, and they made it safely outside. But the fire soon spread and cut off access to those exits. All of the remaining exits were either in the front of the theater, at the main entrance on Washington Street, or through the emergency doors on Flood's Alley.

While the crowd was set in panic mode, head usher Thomas Rochford rushed to the rear of the theater, and he opened the special exit doors on Flood's Alley . Because of Rochford's action, the people on the ground floor were able to exit the theater in less than three minutes. So in effect, the people in the least crowded part of the theater had the fastest escape routes.

However, the open doors on Flood's Alley caused a brisk airflow to blast into the theater, which increased the intensity of the fire.

The people on the second floor had two stairways from which they could escape. The main 7-foot-wide stairway, the stairway in which they had entered the building , led to the vestibule near the Washington Street exit. The other exit was a narrower stairway that led to Flood's Alley.

Most decided to rush for the main stairway, because it was the one they were most familiar with. This caused a logjam of the greatest proportions, since instead of an orderly exit, the people worked themselves into a frenzy. People started getting tangled with each other. Some people jammed into doorways, and others fell forward down the stairs onto the people below them, causing the flow of people out of the building to stop completely.

Sergeant John Cain, from the First Precinct next door, fought his way into the theater and with the help of janitor Van Sicken, he began to untangle the fallen people so that the crowd behind them could get down the stairs to safety. By all accounts, almost all the people from the second floor dress circle seats were able to exit the theater alive. But the people jammed into the gallery on the third floor were doomed from the start, and they knew it.

People started jumping from the family circle seats into the auditorium below. Some were injured so badly from the jump they were not able to exit the theater. Other people lowered themselves from a small third-floor window to Flood's Alley below. One man forced himself through a ventilator shaft which deposited him onto the roof of the police station next door.

But most of the people in the gallery had no way to save themselves. After a few people were able to stumble down the stairway from which they had entered the building to the safety outside, the supports for the gallery collapsed, thrusting hundreds of people three floors down onto the bottom level.

Charles Straub had been sitting in the gallery near the stairway. He was sitting with his friend Joseph Kremer.

Straub said afterwards, "We could hardly run down the stairs;

we were crowded down."

Even though hundreds of people had tripped and fell on top of him, Straub was somehow able to make it down the stairs and out of the theater. He estimated about 25 people from the gallery had made it out before him and about 12 people after him. The rest were trapped inside.

He never saw his friend Kremer again.

Charles Vine had been sitting in the gallery, but far away from the only stairway. He thought about jumping from one of the windows facing Flood's Alley, but it was a 60-foot drop, and he would certainly perish from that jump. So Vine hurried to the front of the gallery, and he decided to jump from there to the dress circle below. Vine cut himself badly on a chair and was knocked out for a moment. But Vine quickly regained consciousness, and he was able to force his way down the second floor stairs to the exit door below.

Fire Marshall Keady said later that he thought Vine had been "the last person to leave the gallery alive."

Fifteen minutes after the fire had begun, the entire interior of the theater was in flames. At 11:45 p.m., the east wall of the theater fell with a loud grumbling, burying more than 300 men, women, and children under tons of bricks and burning debris.

Thomas Nevins, the Chief Engineer of the Brooklyn Fire Department, had arrived at the theater around 11:26 p. m. He immediately saw there was no way to save the theater and that his job was now to confine the fire to that single structure. When the additional fire-fighting equipment arrived just before midnight, Nevins used that equipment to keep adjoining buildings free of sparks and burning debris.

By midnight, around 5,000 spectators had assembled in the streets outside the theater. Some were looking for signs of loved ones who had gone to the theater, but had not yet returned home.

At 1 a.m., the Flood's Alley wall collapsed, and by 3 a.m. the fire had started to burn itself out. At that point, Chief Nevins considered the fire under control. The early newspapers that morning reported the fire, but said that only a handful of people had been killed.

At the break of dawn, Chief Nevins led a contingent of fire personnel into the building. Chief Nevins discovered almost the entire theater had collapsed into the cellar. As the firemen made their way through the ruins, they made a terrible discovery. What appeared to be plain rubbish, was in fact, a mangled mess of charred human bodies. Some of the bodies were intact, and some had missing limbs. All were burned beyond recognition. It was later determined that almost all the dead had been sitting in the third floor gallery when the fire started.

Removal of the bodies took three days. It was a long and tedious project because, in their charred condition, the bodies would immediately fall apart when they were moved.

Forensic science being in its infant stages at the time, an exact body count was impossible. Initial reports in the newspapers said there were anywhere from 275 to 400 fatalities in the Brooklyn Theater Fire. A coroner's report later said there were 283 fatalities, but that was only an educated guess. One hundred and three unidentified bodies and parts of bodies were buried in a common grave at Greenwood Cemetery in Brooklyn.

The death count in the Brooklyn Theater Fire of 1876 was exceeded only by the Iroquois Theater fire which occurred on December 30, 1903, in Chicago, Ill, where at least 605 people died, and the Cocoanut Grove nightclub fire in Boston, on November 28, 1942, which killed 492 people.

The Brooklyn Theater Fire of 1876 did spur New York City to institute safeguards that reduced the possibility of a similar fire ever happening again. Changes in the building code barred the presence of paints, woods, and construction material in the stage area. The code also mandated the use of a solid brick proscenium wall, "extending from the cellar to the roof, to minimize the risk of a stage fire spreading into the auditorium."

Other changes to the code decreed that "proscenium arches were to be equipped with non-flammable fire curtains." Other openings in the proscenium wall required self-closing, fire-resistant doors. And heat-activated sprinkling systems were required for the fly space above the stage.

Starting in the early 1900s, a half hour before the scheduled performance each theater was to have a "Theater Detail Officer" on duty. Before the play started, the Theater Detail Officer's job was to "test the fire alarms, inspect firewall doors, and the fire curtain." During the performance, the theater Detail Officer would "roam the theater, making sure that aisles, hallways, and fire exits were clear and accessible to all patrons."

There were contradicting accounts about what happened to Kate Claxton after she escaped from the Brooklyn Theater Fire. One newspaper said she was seen sitting safely in the First Precinct police station one hour after the fire. Another report said that three hours after the fire had started, a New York City newspaper reporter found Claxton wandering in a daze at Manhattan's City Hall. Her hands and face were bloated with burn blisters, and she could not remember taking the ferry from Brooklyn to Manhattan.

Scant months later, after Claxton had recovered from her injuries, she traveled to St. Louis to appear in another play. As soon as she arrived in St. Louis, she checked into the Southern Hotel. In hours, that hotel went up in flames. But Claxton and her brother, whom she was traveling with, made a miraculous escape seconds before the hotel collapsed.

This effectively ended Kate Claxton's theatrical career. Fearing she was some kind of a jinx, other actors refused to appear on stage with her. And theatergoers, fearing another fire, boycotted her performances altogether.

Nine years after the Brooklyn Theater Fire, Kate Claxton shared her thoughts with the *New York Times*.

She said, "We thought we were acting for the best in continuing the play as we did, with the hope that the fire would be put out without difficulty, or that the audience would leave gradually or quietly. But the result proved that it was not the right course. The curtain should have been kept down until the flames had been extinguished, or if it had been found impossible to cope with them, the audience should have been calmly informed that indisposition on the part of some member of the company, or some unfortunate occurrence behind the scenery compelled a suspension of the performance, and they should have been requested to disperse as quietly as they could. Raising the curtain created a draft which fanned the flames into fury."

Hindsight is 20/20, but Kate Claxton's later observations were absolutely correct. The Brooklyn Theater Fire of 1876 could have produced minimal damage, if only the theater personnel had not bumbled, but had acted in a coherent, methodical, and calm manner.

Sadly, this never happened.

The General Slocum Steamship Disaster of 1904

If you ask New Yorkers, besides the bombing of the World Trade
Center Towers on September 11, 2001, what was the biggest disaster
in New York City history, most would say the Triangle Shirtwaist
Factory Fire of 1911, which killed 141 people, mostly women.
However, by far the worst tragedy ever to take place in New York
City besides 9/11 was the now-forgotten 1904 *General Slocum*
paddle boat disaster, in which more than 1000 German people,
mostly woman and children, perished in an accident that certainly
could have been prevented.

Starting in the 1840s, tens of thousands of German immigrants
began flooding the Lower East Side of Manhattan, which is now
called Alphabet City, but what was then called the Kleindeutschland,
or Little Germany. Just in the 1850s alone over 800,000 Germans
came to America, and by 1855, New York City had the third-largest
German population of any city in the world.

The German immigrants were different than the Irish
immigrants who, due to the Irish potato famine in Ireland, were also
emigrating to New York City at a fast pace during the middle part of
the 19th century. Whereas the Irish were mostly lower-class laborers,
the Germans were better educated and possessed skills that made
them obtain a higher rung on the economic ladder than did the Irish.
More than half the bakers in New York City were of German
descent, and most cabinet makers in New York City were either
German, or of German descent. Germans were also very active in the
construction business, which at the time was very profitable because
of all the large buildings being built in New York City during the
mid-to-late 1800s.

Joseph Wedemeyer, Oswald Ottendorfer, and Friedrich Sorge
were New York City German-Americans who were extremely active
in the creation and growth of trade unions. In New York City,
German-American clubs, which were called Vereins, were highly
involved in politics. Ottendorfer owned and edited the *Staats-
Zeitung,* the largest German-American newspaper in town. He
became such a force in politics, that in 1861, he was instrumental,
through his German Democracy political club, in getting New York
City Mayor Fernando Wood elected for his second term. In 1863,

Ottendorfer propelled another German, Godfrey Gunther, to succeed Wood as mayor.

Little Germany reached its peak in the 1870s. It then encompassed over 400 blocks, comprised of six avenues and 40 streets, running south from 14th Street to Houston Street and from the Bowery east to the East River. Tompkins Square, and its park, was considered the epicenter of Little Germany. The park itself was called the *Weisse Garten*, where Germans congregated daily to discuss what was important to their lives and livelihoods.

Avenue B was called the German Broadway, where almost every building contained a first-floor store or a workshop marketing every sort of commodity that was desired by the German populace. Avenue A was known for its beer gardens, oyster saloons, and assorted grocery stores. In Little Germany there were also sporting clubs, libraries, choirs, shooting clubs, factories, department stores, German theaters, German schools, German churches, and German synagogues for the German Jews.

Starting around 1880, the wealthier Germans began moving out of New York City to the suburbs. And by the turn of the 20th Century, the German population in Little Germany had shrunk to around 50,000 people, still a sizable amount for any ethnic group in New York City.

On June 15, 1904, St. Mark's Evangelical Lutheran Church on 6th Street charted the paddle boat *General Slocum,* for the sum of $350, to take members of its congregation to its yearly picnic celebrating the end of the school year. At a few minutes after 9 a.m., more than 1,300 people boarded the *General Slocum*. Their destination was the Locust Grove on Long Island Sound, where they expected to enjoy a day of swimming, games, and the best of German food.

The *General Slocum,* owned by the Knickerbocker Steamship Company, was named for Civil War officer and New York Congressman Henry Warner Slocum. It was built by the W. & A. Fletcher Company of Hoboken, New Jersey, and was a side-wheel paddle boat powered by a single-cylinder, surface-condensing, vertical-beam steam engine, with 53-inch bore and 12-foot stroke. Each wheel had 26 paddles and was 31 feet in diameter. Her maximum speed was about 16 knots.

Almost from the day of its launching in 1891, the *General*

Slocum suffered one mishap after another. Four months after her launching, the *General Slocum* ran aground near the Rockaways. Several tugboats were needed to drag the *General Slocum* back into the water.

It was an exceptionally bad year for the *General Slocum* in 1894. On June 29, the *General Slocum* was returning from the Rockaways with 4,700 passengers. Suddenly, it struck a sandbar so hard her electrical generator blew out. In August, during a terrible rain storm, the *General Slocum* ran aground a second time, this time near Coney Island. The passengers had to be transferred to another boat in order to make their way back home. The next month the *General Slocum* hit the trifecta when it collided with the tug boat *R. T. Sayre* in the middle of the East River. In this incident, the *General Slocum's* steering was severely damaged, and it had to be repaired. The *General Slocum* was accident-free until July of 1898, when the *General Slocum* collided with the *Amelia* near Battery Park.

On August 17, 1901, the *General Slocum* was carrying, what was described as "900 intoxicated Patterson Anarchists." Suddenly, some of the passengers started to riot, and others tried to physically take control of the boat by storming the bridge. However, the crew fought off the rioters and were able to keep control of the boat. When the captain docked at the police pier, 17 "anarchists" were arrested.

Finally, in June of 1902, the *General Slocum* ran aground again. The boat was unable to be freed, so its passengers had to camp out the entire night until reinforcements could arrive the following morning. The captain of the boat in that incident was none other than William H. Van Schaick, the same man who would be the chief officer of the *General Slocum* on its fateful voyage.

On June 15, 1904, about 15 minutes after the *General Slocum* left the pier at East Third Street, it was even with East 125th Street. At this point, Captain Van Schaick was notified by one of his crew that a fire had started in the Lamp Room, in the forward section of the boat. The fire was probably ignited by a discarded cigarette or a match, and it had been obviously fueled by the straw, oily rags, and lamp oil strewn around the room. The Captain had also been told there was a fire on board a few minutes earlier by a 12-year-old boy, but Captain Van Schaick did not believe the boy. Other people on board said the fire had started almost simultaneously in several locations, including a paint locker filled with flammable fluids and a cabin filled with gasoline.

This is where Captain Van Schaick made a terrible mistake in judgment.

Since land was close by, all the Captain had to do was run his ship aground before the flames spread any further. Then he could unload his passengers, mostly woman and children, quickly, before there were any fatalities. But for some reason Captain Van Schaick decided to head straight into a headwind and try to land his boat at North Brother Island, just off the southern shore of the Bronx. Captain Van Schaick would later say the reason for his decision was that he was trying to prevent the fire from spreading on land to riverside buildings and oil tanks. But by going into heavy headwinds, he was actually fanning the fire.

Captain Van Schaick later said at his trial, "I started to head to 134th Street, but was warned off by the captain of a tugboat, who shouted to me that the boat would set fire to the lumber yards and oil tanks there. Besides, I knew that the shore was lined with rocks and the boat would founder if I put in there. I then fixed upon North Brother Island."

As the boat chugged onward, passengers ran in panic around the deck. Mothers were looking for their children. Fathers were looking for their families. Young boys and girls scrambled onto the deck chairs, waving frantically for help at the crowds who had assembled on the shore. The flames increased by the second, accelerated by the boat's fresh coat of highly flammable paint.

At this point, overcome by smoke inhalation and with the flames flickering at their torsos, feet and faces, people began jumping into the water. Some were rescued by boats which had rushed near the fiery *General Slocum*. But most of the woman and girls who jumped, because of the bulky woman's clothing of that era, quickly drowned. Some people died when the floors of the boat collapsed. Others were beaten to death by the still-churning paddles, as they flung themselves over the sides of the boat towards the water.

People who tried to use the life jackets on board were in for a horrible surprise.

Although there were 3,000 life jackets available, they were all but useless. The vast majority were rotted out, with the cork inside the jackets used for buoyancy almost entirely disintegrated. The people who donned the life jackets and plunged into the water, immediately sank like rocks. Some people tried to dislodge the emergency lifeboats, but they failed to do so because the lifeboats were firmly wired in place.

People on the shore saw a girl in a blue dress jump off the side of the boat. They watched in horror as the girl hit the wooden paddle wheel. The wheel churned violently, dragging the girl under it. The people on shore could hear the screaming girl's frail body being thrashed about like a rag doll by the paddle wheel, before her screaming stopped, and she disappeared into the murky waters. A little boy, clutching his stuffed toy dog, was thrown into the river by his weeping mother. The boy was fished from the river alive, still squeezing his precious toy dog.

Sixteen-year-old Albert Frese was one of the lucky ones who survived the *General Slocum* disaster. Frese, at the time, was a mail clerk in the Funk and Wagnalls publishing house. As horrified people scampered all around him, Frese hurried to the stern of the burning boat.

According to Edward Ross Ellis's *The Epic of New York City*, "Frese jumped feet first, with his ankles together and his arms rigid at his side. He was able to swim safely to shore, and later he became treasurer of his firm."

As Captain Van Schaick resolutely and pigheadedly steered his boat onward, people on Manhattan's east shore were now running frantically along the riverbank trying to keep pace with the burning boat. Others were mobilized in wagons and carts, and screaming for the Captain to run his boat ashore. Some people flung barrels into the river for the people floundering in the water to use as makeshift life preservers. Small boats tried to chase down the *General Slocum* from behind, but they were unable to do so. However, some of these boats were able to fish the better swimmers out of the water and bring them safely to shore.

Despite this utter mayhem and the pleading of the people on the shore to run his boat aground, Captain Van Schaick, his own clothes on fire, ignored them and continued toward North Brother Island. When Captain Van Schaick finally beached his boat at North Brother Island, the boat was one huge fireball.

Captain Van Schaick said later, "I stuck to my post in the pilothouse until my cap caught fire. We were then about twenty-five feet off North Brother Island. She went on the beach; bow on, in about twenty-five feet of water. . . . Most of the people aft, where the fire raged fiercest, jumped in when we were in deep water, and were carried away. We had no chance to lower the lifeboats. They were burned before the crew could get at them."

At North Brother Island, nurses, doctors, and even the patients in the island's contagious disease hospital, rushed to help the survivors. Some carried ladders, which they used to guide the survivors, most badly burned, down from the boat. Others caught little children who were heaved down to them by hysterical parents. Within minutes, all the survivors, including the captain and several crew members, were taken safely away from the flaming boat and admitted to the hospital.

From his hospital window, a feverish measles patient saw the horror transpiring in front of him. He summoned the courage, hurried from the hospital, and sprinted into the water. He was able to save several children.

A nurse who couldn't swim dashed into the river to grab several children. She did this repeatedly, when suddenly the tide pulled her into deeper water. Incredibly, the nurse found out she could indeed swim, and she continued rescuing whomever she could reach.

City Health Commissioner Thomas Darlington was present on North Brother Island the day the fiery *General Slocum* ran aground.

"I will never be able to forget the scene, the utter horror of it," Darlington said. "The patients in the contagious wards, especially in the scarlet fever ward, went wild at things they saw from their windows and went screaming and beating at the doors, until it took fifty nurses and doctors to quiet them. They were all locked up. Along the beach the boats were carrying in the living and dying, and towing in the dead."

When the fire first started, someone rang the city desk of the *World* on Park Row. The man, who didn't identify himself, told the newspaper editor that he was in his office at 137th Street, and he could see the burning boat from his office window. The editor immediately contacted Eugene Moran, who owned a tugboat company at 134th Street. Moran told the editor that he had no tugboats available in that area, but that it would be faster anyway to send his men by elevated train from the Park Row station to the Morris Park station in the north Bronx. The editor ordered his men onto the train, and as a result, the *World* had the story of the tragedy before any other New York City daily newspaper.

When the *World* reporters arrived on the scene, they were overcome by grief. As the boat was enveloped in smoke and flames, the reporters and the *World's* photographers spotted dozens of blackened and bloody dead bodies scattered along the shoreline. As the photographers snapped away and the reporters jotted down their notes, several hardened newspapermen broke down in tears. Then they rushed to find phones so that they could deliver their stories to the rewrite men at their newspaper. Their description of the tragedy on the phones were so graphic, when the rewrite men heard what had transpired, some rushed into the men's room to vomit.

The *New York Times* reported the following day, "On the night of June 15, 1904, grief-crazed crowds lined the shore where the bodies were being brought in by the boatload. Scores were prevented from throwing themselves into the river."

The police released a report a few days later claiming that 1,031 people had perished in the *General Slocum* fire. For the next few weeks, police divers searched for bodies in the partially sunk remains of the *General Slocum*. Police and rescue parties scoured the banks of the river for miles in both directions looking for bodies.

On the night of the fire, scores of husbands came home from work only to discover that their entire families had perished in the fire. Some committed suicide, others went mad, and some later died of grief. For three days, hearses transversed the streets of Little Germany carrying bodies and parts of bodies to their graves in Lutheran Cemetery in Middle Village, Queens.

A Federal grand jury indicted eight people as a result of the disaster. Those people included Captain Van Schaick, two boat inspectors, and the president, secretary, treasurer, and commodore of the Knickerbocker Steamship Company.

However, only Captain Van Schaick was convicted at trial. The Captain was convicted of criminal negligence, and failing to maintain proper fire drills and fire extinguishers. There was a hung jury on the manslaughter charge. Captain Van Schaick was sentenced to 10 years in prison. The Captain served three-and-a-half years at Sing Sing Prison before he received parole. On August 26, 1911, the administration of President William Howard Taft voted to release Captain Van Schaick from parole. And on December 19,

1912, President Taft pardoned the Captain, who died in 1927.

The Knickerbocker Steamship Company received a ridiculously small fine, even though there was sufficient evidence that they had falsified inspection records. The sunken remains of the *General Slocum* were raised to the surface and subsequently converted into a barge, which predictably sank during a storm in 1911.

The tragedy of the *General Slocum* forced a major reconstruction of steamboat safety regulations. A week after the fire, President Theodore Roosevelt ordered a five-man commission to investigate why the tragedy had occurred and what could be done to prevent it from happening again. The commission was especially tough on the United States Steamboat Inspection Service (USSIS), which had failed miserably at their job of ensuring steamboat safety. Dozens of USSIS employees were fired, and new inspections of all steamboats were ordered. Not surprisingly, numerous violations were found, running from useless life jackets to rotted fire hoses.

The five-man committee recommended many reforms, including fireproof metal bulkheads to contain fires, steam pipes extending from the boiler into cargo areas (to act as a sprinkler), improved life jackets (one for each passenger and crew member), fire hoses capable of handling 100 pounds of pressure per square inch and accessible life boats. All these reforms were immediately instituted, which dramatically improved steamboat safety.

The *General Slocum* fire all but erased the German population from the Lower East Side of Manhattan. Soon after the *General Slocum* fire, because memories of the tragedy were too horrible to endure, hundreds of German families moved out of the Lower East Side of Manhattan. Some settled in the Upper East Side's Yorkville section, creating a new Germantown. Some moved to Astoria in Queens and others left New York City completely.

Strangely, the memory of *General Slocum* fire, even though it killed almost ten times as many people as did the Triangle Shirtwaist Factory Fire of 1911, quickly faded from the general public's consciousness. A large part of the reason was that the onset of World War One removed all sympathies for anyone of German descent and all of the victims of the *General Slocum* fire were German.

In 1905, the Sympathy Society of German Ladies commissioned sculptor Bruno Louis Zimm to design a memorial fountain, which was unveiled on May 30, 1905 at the northwestern corner of

Tompkins Square Park. This white 9-foot fountain is sculpted of pink Tennessee marble. On the front, above the carved lion's head spout and basin, there is a depiction of two innocent children staring off towards the sea, with the inscription, "They were earth's purest children, loving and fair."

The memorial fountain still stands in Tompkins Square Park to this very day.

The Triangle Shirtwaist Factory Fire - 1911

If it weren't for the greed of the sweatshop bosses, this tragedy may never have occurred. However, on March 25, 1911, the Triangle Shirtwaist Factory Fire took the lives of 141 people, most of them women.

At the turn of the 20th century, working conditions in the New York City sweatshops were abysmal. Men, woman, and children toiled in dirty factories, warehouses, and tenements, doing menial tasks that made the garment industry one of the most profitable businesses in the nation. Labor laws were inadequate and hardly ever enforced. Factory inspections were rare, and if they were done at all, the factory owners knew whose palms to grease to get high inspection marks, when the condemnation of their factory was the proper course of action.

In 1899, a law banning night work for women was declared unconstitutional. The absurd reason given by the courts, whose members were often in the sweatshop boss's back pockets, was that the law "deprived woman of the liberty to work in factories at night, or for as long as they wished to." In 1907, this ruling was upheld by the New York Court of Appeals. Even though the International Ladies Garment Workers Union was formed in 1900, the sweatshop bosses hired thugs as strikebreakers, to keep the union in line, by force if necessary.

Of all the greedy sweatshop owners, the worst offenders were Max Blanck and Isaac Harris, who owned the Triangle Shirtwaist Company, located on the 8th, 9th, and 10th floors of the 10-story Asch Building at 22 Washington Place, on the corner of Greene Street. The factory produced women's blouses, known at the time as "shirtwaists." The firm employed around 500-600 people, most of whom were young female Jewish and Italian immigrants, who worked under horrible conditions, for 9 hours a day on weekdays, and 7 hours on Saturdays. The bosses were such tyrants, they charged their employees for needles and for other supplies. They also charged them a fee for using their chairs, and if one of the employees damaged a piece of goods, they had to pay three times the value of the item to replace it.

In 1908, Blanck and Harris formed a sham company union that

served their purposes much better than it served their hundreds of employees. Several employees, who tried to join a legitimate union, like the International Ladies Garment Workers Union or the United Hebrew Trades, were quickly fired. The reason management gave for these firings was that because of poor economic conditions, they had to cut staff. Yet strangely enough, new workers were hired almost immediately after the dismissal of the others.

Because Triangle Shirtwaist Company had locked out their dismissed workers, Local 25 of the International Ladies Garment Workers Union called for a strike against them. Blanck and Harris hired union strike breakers, or "schlammers," to beat up the male pickets. They also hired prostitutes to mingle with the female workers in the picket lines, in order to cause disruptions. The police and the judges, obviously working at the behest of the owners, sided with Blanck and Harris. One judge even said at the sentencing of one picketer, "You are on strike against God."

On March 25, 1911, it was a cold and windy day. As the 5p.m. closing time approached, it was estimated that 600 employees, packed in like sardines, were working at the sewing machine at the Triangle Shirtwaist Company. Most were women between the ages of 13 and 23. The 5p.m. bell rang, and the women scrambled to get their coats and hats, and then they rushed for the elevators.

Suddenly, a fire broke out on the southeast corner of the 8th floor. It was later determined that the fire was inadvertently caused by a cigarette butt that had been thrown into a litter basket, near a sewing machine. An updraft of air sent the flames and smoke shooting upwards towards the roof.

The building had no sprinkler system, and the fire quickly enveloped the entire 8th, 9th, and 10th floors. Girls on the 8th floor ran to a stairwell on the Washington Place side of the building, but the door was locked from the outside. The fire was so intense, all the windows on the top three floors of the building blew out from the heat.

Some workers were able to jam themselves into the elevators, while the elevators were still working. Others, including Blanck and Harris, were saved because they were able to make it to the safety of the roof.

A passerby named Joe Zito, and an elevator operator named Gaspar Mortillalo, used the only working elevator to make five trips up to the 9th floor; taking down 25-30 terrified people at a time. However, that elevator soon became inoperable too.

Within five minutes, the fire trucks had arrived, but there was not much they could do. Their extension ladders only reached the 6th floor and the stream from their hoses only reached the 7th floor. Rather than burn to death, people began jumping out of the windows, sometimes in groups of two, three, and four.

A man and a woman appeared in a 9th floor window, their clothes ablaze. They kissed, then hugged, and jumped together, their bodies smashing on the cold pavement below.

The firemen brought out safety nets to catch the jumpers, but it was hopeless.

One fire chief later said, "Life nets? What good were life nets? The little ones went right through the life nets, and the pavement too. Nobody could hold a life net when those girls from the ninth floor came down."

The fire only lasted 10 minutes, but when it was over, 141 workers had died; 125 were women.

Nine months after the fire, Blanck and Harris were put on trial on manslaughter charges. However, the trial, like the earlier building inspections, was a farce. The judge was Thomas Crain, a Tammany Hall appointee, and he had little interest in justice for the dead workers. Judge Crain manipulated a trial where only an acquittal was possible. It took the jury just 100 minutes to render a verdict of not-guilty.

This did not go down too well with the victim's families. The day after the not-guilty verdicts, hundreds of despondent victim's relatives stood outside the Tombs Courthouse. Blanck and Harris, surrounded by five police officers, tried to slither out of the building through the Leonard Street exit. When the two men were spotted, they were quickly enveloped by an angry crowd.

David Weiner, whose sister had died in the fire, charged at the sweatshop bosses, swinging his fist in the air.

"Not Guilty? Not Guilty?" Weiner screamed. "It was murder! Murder!"

Weiner quickly was subdued by the police, but he was so distraught, he fainted and had to be rushed to the hospital.

In 1913, the victim's families won a lawsuit against Blanck and Harris. The families were awarded a measly $75 per victim, whereas

Blanck and Harris were paid by the insurance company $60,000 more than the total reported loss of life and property. Ironically, in late 1913, Blanck was arrested again, for locking the doors to his sweatshop.

The tragedy of the Triangle Shirtwaist Factory Fire did not go for naught.

The New York State Legislature - whose members included future Presidential candidate Al Smith, and Robert Wagner, the father of the future Mayor of New York City by the same name - forced the state to completely rewrite its labor laws. The State Legislature created the New York State Factory Investigating Committee, to "investigate factory conditions in this and other cities, and to report remedial measures of legislation to prevent hazard, or loss of life, among employees through fire, insanitary conditions, and occupational diseases."

As a direct result of the Triangle Shirtwaist Factory Fire, The American Society of Safety Engineers was founded on October 14, 1911.

Part 4 – Crooked Politicians

The dates after the names of the crooked politicians names denote the times they held the office they so disgraced.

*****

Mayor Fernando Wood – 1857-1862

In 1857, it was chaotic times in New York City, as the city's two adversarial police forces battled over the right to arrest people, and to accept graft from anyone willing and able to pay.

In 1853, under Democratic Mayor Harper, the first uniformed police force in New York City was created. Their uniform consisted of a blue coat with brass buttons, a blue cap, and gray pants. Led by Police Chief George G. Matsell, the police were generally more crooked than the crooks, taking bribes not to arrest people and sometimes taking bribes *to* arrest people. The citizens of New York City complained that their police force, called the Municipal Police, was "the worse in the world."

By the age of 37, Fernando Wood was a millionaire in the real estate business. On January 1, 1855, after buying votes through his wealth, Wood was elected Mayor of New York City. Wood immediately inserted himself as head of the police graft-gravy-train; charging new police captains $200 a year for a promotion to their $1,000-a-year job. Of course, to make up for the shortfall, the police captains charged each patrolman under their command $40 a year. The policemen, in turn, shook down honest citizens and protected dishonest citizens for pay, so everyone on the public law enforcement dole was quite happy to keep things just the way they were.

However, the New York State Legislature would have none of that.

In 1857, the legislature passed an act creating a new Metropolitan Police Force, with Fredrick Tallmadge named as Superintendent of the Force. The legislature also ordered Wood to immediately disband his 1,100 member Municipal Police Force. Wood refused; saying the creation of the new police force was unconstitutional. Thus, the court battle began over which police force would be the one to patrol New York City.

The Supreme Court soon voted that the creation of the new police force was indeed constitutional. Yet Wood, with the backing of Police Chief Matsell, steadfastly refused to cooperate. Eight hundred men, all aligned with the Democratic Party, stayed with Wood and Matsell. However, three hundred men, under respected Police Captain George W. Walling, defected and comprised the new Metropolitan Police Force, which was backed by the Republican Party.

On June 16, 1857, the issue came to a head. The street commissioner Joseph Taylor had died, and Wood, for the sum of $50,000, appointed Charles Devlin as the new street commissioner. On the same day, Republican Governor John A. King appointed Daniel Conover to the same position. As Conover entered City Hall to assume his new post, Wood had his Municipal Police throw Conover out of the building. Conover immediately went to a Republican judge, who swore out two warrants for Wood's arrest: one for assault and one for inciting to riot.

Captain Walling strode to City Hall to arrest Wood on the assault charge, but he was met by a contingent of five hundred Municipals. Captain Walling was allowed to enter the building and Wood's office. However, when Captain Walling told Wood he was under arrest for assault, Wood refused to recognize the legality of the arrest warrant.

Captain Walling grabbed Wood's arm to lead him out of the building, but he was immediately swarmed by 20 Municipals and thrown out of City Hall himself. Captain Walling repeatedly tried to go back up the steps of City Hall, but he was beaten back every time.

Suddenly, a contingent of one hundred Metropolitan Police, wearing their new uniforms of frock coats, and plug hats, arrived to serve the second arrest warrant on Wood. Instead of wearing the gold badges of the Municipals, the Mets wore copper badges, which gave birth to the term "coppers," and then "cops."

The motley Metropolitan Police were described by essayist G.T. Strong as, "a miscellaneous assortment of suckers, soaplocks, Irishmen and Plug-Uglies (an Irish Street Gang)."

Thus, began a horrendous half-hour battle between the two New York City Police Departments. The Mets were vastly outnumbered by the Municipals, and when the fight was over, some Mets were lucky enough to be able to flee unharmed. However, 53 Mets were injured, 12 hurt seriously, and one was crippled for life.

While the fighting was intensifying, Captain Walling rushed over the office of Sheriff J.J.V. Westervelt, and he implored the sheriff to arrest Mayor Wood. After consulting with a state attorney, Captain Walling, Sheriff Westervelt, and the state attorney marched to City Hall, and they pushed their way into Wood's office.

When the three men informed Wood he was indeed under arrest, he shouted at them, "I will never let you arrest me!"

At the same time, a beaten contingent of Mets spotted the Seventh Regiment of the National Guard boarding a boat for Boston. The Mets convinced the National Guard that they were needed to police a state matter.

Recognizing the severity of the situation, Major General Charles Sandford marched his men to City Hall. As his troops stood guard, Sandford strode up the steps of City Hall and into Wood's office, where he announced to Wood that he was under arrest. Wood looked out the window and spotted the National Guard. Realizing his men were no match for the military troops, Wood finally submitted to the arrest.

Yet, this was only the beginning of a long strife. For the rest of the summer, the two police departments constantly conflicted. When a Met cop arrested a crook, a Municipal would step in and set the man free. And vice versa. On numerous occasions, contingents of policemen would raid the other department's station house and free all the prisoners.

In the meantime, the criminals of New York City were having a field day.

While the two police forces battled each other all hours of the day and night, honest citizens were being robbed while walking the streets. Murders were committed with impunity, and still, all the two police departments were interested in was fighting each other.

This total indifference by the two New York City police departments led to a two-day riot on July 4 and July 5, of 1857, when the Bowery Boys and the Dead Rabbits street gangs squared off with fists, knives, stones, and pistols. As many as a thousand gang members were involved. Hundreds were injured, and several gang members were killed. The riots also led to the indiscriminate looting of stores, in the Five Points and Bowery areas and as far north as 14ᵗʰ Street.

Finally, in the fall of 1857, the Court of Appeals upheld the Supreme Court's ruling, that the Metropolitan Police were the only legitimate police department in town. The Municipals were disbanded, and although Mayor Wood had been arrested, he was released on bond and never tried.

The Mets, who were injured in the June 16 fight, sued Mayor Wood for personal damages. They were awarded $250 apiece by the courts, but Mayor Wood refused to pay a dime. Finally, the city of New York was forced to pay the damages from the city treasury, including the injured Mets' legal costs.

Wood was defeated in the 1858 Mayoral race by Daniel F. Tiemann. Yet, in 1860, the rotten Wood was somehow re-elected mayor of New York City, until 1862.

After the Civil War started, Wood floated a trial balloon, whereby New York City would secede from the state of New York, which was run by Republicans, and therefore, become a free city. Wood's proposal was shot down, and *New York Tribune's* editor Horace Greeley, wrote in an editorial, "Fernando Wood evidently wants to be a traitor. It is lack of courage only that makes him content with being a blackguard."

In 1867, Wood found his true calling in the United States House of Representatives, where he served, not too admirably, until his death on February 14, 1881.

A year later, statesman and author John Bigelow, who knew Wood well, said that Wood was, "The most corrupt man who ever sat in the mayor's chair of New York City."

William "Boss" Tweed - 1850-1973

William "Boss" Tweed, head crook at Tammany Hall, stole so much money from the New York City coffers, by 1870 Tweed had become the third largest land owner in the entire city.

Tweed, a third generation Scottish-Irishman, was born on April 3, 1823, at 24 Cherry Street on the Lower East Side of Manhattan. His father was a chair maker, and the young Tweed tried to follow in his father's footsteps, but the lure of the streets became too much for Tweed to overcome. Tweed ran with a motley crew of juvenile delinquents called the "Cherry Street Gang," who wreaked havoc on local merchants by stealing their wares and selling them on the street's black market.

Soon, Tweed became boss of the "Cherry Hill Gang," and he (as did most gang members of that era) joined various volunteer fire companies, which were a springboard for men with political ambitions. Tweed helped found American Fire Engine Company No. 6, which was called the "Big Six." During his time in the volunteer fire business, Tweed forged friendships with people of all ancestries: Irish, Scottish, Germans - anyone who could help him climb the ladder of public service, with only one thing in mind, steal big and steal often.

In 1850, Tweed ran unsuccessfully for assistant alderman on the Democratic ticket. However, a year later Tweed was elected alderman, a non-paying job, but with unlimited power for anyone smart enough, and crooked enough, to take advantage of its perks. Just scant weeks after he became an alderman, Tweed brokered a deal to buy land on Wards Island for a new potter's field. The asking price was $30,000, but Tweed paid $103,450 of the city's money for the land, then split the difference between himself and several other civic-minded officials.

In 1855, Tweed was elected to the New York City Board of Elections, which was another cash cow for the money-hungry Tweed. He sold city textbooks for his own profit, and he sold teachers' jobs to whomever had the money to buy one. In one instance, Tweed peddled a teachers' position to a crippled schoolmarm for $75, even though the job only paid $300 a year.

In 1857, Tweed was appointed to the New York County Board of Supervisors, which propelled Tweed into a much more profitable form of thievery. Tweed formed what was known as the "Tweed Ring," which was nothing more than Tweed and his buddies controlling every job and work permit in the entire city of New York. Every contractor, artisan, and merchant who wanted to do business with the city had to cough up the cash, and they coughed up plenty. It is estimated that Tweed's Board of Supervisors pocketed 15 percent of every dollar spent on construction in New York City.

Concerning Tweed and his cronies, American lawyer and diarist George Templeton Strong wrote in 1860, "Our city government is rotten to the core."

By 1865, Tweed's wealth had grown to impressive proportions and so did his girth. Standing 5-feet-11-inches, Tweed's weight ballooned to 320 pounds. His reputation for eating was legendary, and he consumed enormous amounts of the finest foods in the finest restaurants. Tweed floundered around town, like a whale out of water, with a huge diamond stuck right in the middle of his fancy shirt, flouting his tremendous wealth.

It is estimated, from 1865 to 1871, Tweed's gang stole as much as $200 million from the New York City Treasury. They did this by over-billing the city for everything imaginable. They paid out of the city's coffers $10,000 for $75 worth of pencils, $171,000 for $4,000 worth of tables and chairs, and $1,826,000 for the plastering of a municipal building, which actually cost only $50,000 to plaster. Tweed also gave citizenship to over 60,000 immigrants, none of whom could read or write, but who could vote for Tweed and his cohorts on election day.

Tweed's downfall began on December 25, 1869, when *Harper's Weekly* published a cartoon of Tweed and his gang breaking into a huge box, with the caption "Taxpayers' and Tenants' Hard Earned Cash."

Upon seeing the cartoon, Tweed said, "Stop them damned pictures. I don't care so much what the papers say about me. My constituents don't know how to read, but they can't help seeing them damned pictures!"

With the pressure mounting to unveil the extent of Tweed's corruption, a blue ribbon panel, headed by future Presidential candidate Samuel J. Tilden, was formed to investigate New York

City's financial documents. When the books were checked, it was discovered that money had gone directly from city contractors into Tweed's pocket. The next day, Boss Tweed was arrested.

His first trial, in January 1873, ended in a hung jury; a jury many people thought was bought with Tweed's money. However, in November of that same year, Tweed was convicted on 204 out of 220 counts and sentenced to 12 years in prison.

Tweed was incarcerated in the Ludlow Street Jail, but, for some unknown reason, he was allowed home visits. During one such visit, Tweed fled the country and traveled to Spain, where he worked as a seaman on a commercial ship. Because his picture had been seen frequently in the newspapers, Tweed was recognized and returned to America. Tweed again was imprisoned in the Ludlow Street Jail, but this time no home visits were allowed.

On April 12, 1878, Boss Tweed died in the Ludlow Street Jail from a severe case of pneumonia. He was buried in Brooklyn's Greenwood Cemetery, and due to Tweed's outlandish treachery, New York Mayor Smith Ely would not allow the City Hall flag to be flown at half-mast in Tweed's memory.

No one could account for what became of Boss Tweed's vast amounts of ill-gotten gains. And not surprisingly, there were no reports of a Wells Fargo stagecoach following his horse-drawn hearse.

John Morrissey – "Old Smoke" - 1867-1871

John Morrissey started out as a feared bare-knuckle boxer, but later became a street-gang member and a leg-breaker for the Tammany Hall politicians.

Morrissey was born in Templemore, County Tipperary, Ireland in 1831. The famed potato famine was in its infancy, but Morrissey's parents saw the writing on the wall. They immigrated to America in 1833 and settled in Troy, New York. Not being educated, but good with his fists, Morrissey was relegated to working as a collection agent for the local Irish crime bosses. While working as a bouncer in a Troy brothel, Morrissey taught himself how to read and write. Realizing his future was limited in Troy, Morrissey made the short trek to New York City. There, Morrissey made a name for himself as a rough hooligan, fighting often in bars and on the piers, just for sport.

One day, Morrissey engaged in an impromptu fight with Tom McCann, at the indoor pistol gallery under the St. Charles Hotel. McCann was getting the best of Morrissey, when a powerful McCann punch drove Morrissey over burning coals from a hot stove, which had been overturned during the fight. Morrissey's clothes and flesh were on fire, and with smoke comes from his backside, Morrissey leaped forward, and he immediately battered McCann senseless. Hence, Morrissey was awarded the nickname "Old Smoke."

After winning a few more battles, inside and outside the ring, Morrissey challenged world heavyweight champion Yankee Sullivan to a fight for the World's Heavyweight Title. The fight took place on October 12, 1853, at Boston Corners, on the border of Massachusetts and New York. Morrissey was battered throughout the fight, but he won by disqualification in the 37th round, when Sullivan hit Morrissey while he was down.

Buoyed by his newfound fistic fame, and now a member of the Dead Rabbits, a feared street gang, Morrissey was hired by the Democrats from Tammany Hall to protect the polling places from the Bowery Boy's gang, led by Butcher Bill Poole. Poole and his pals terrorized the polling places on election days, in favor of the Native American, or Know-Nothing political party.

On Election Day 1854, Poole announced that he and 30 of his Bowery Boys were headed to a certain local election site to destroy the ballot boxes. Tammany Hall called on Morrissey to protect their interests, and with John A. Kennedy, who later became New York City's Superintendent of Police, they assembled a gang of over 50 Dead Rabbits. Itching for a fight, they stood in wait inside the polling place for Poole and his gang's arrival.

A man of his word, Poole arrived at the polling place looking to do as much damage as possible. However, as Poole scanned the inside of the polling place, he immediately realized his group was vastly outnumbered by Morrissey and the Dead Rabbits.

Not a good thing for Poole.

Poole met Morrissey in the center of the room, and after staring menacingly at each other for a few moments, without saying a word, Poole abruptly turned and left, taking his gang with him. Tammany Hall was so overjoyed by Morrissey's heroics, they gave him a free gambling house (under the protection of the New York City police, of course).

In 1855, Morrissey challenged Poole to a bare-knuckles fight, on a pier near Christopher Street. Poole accepted, but once the two men squared off, instead of fighting with his fists, Poole tried to crush Morrissey to death by squeezing Morrissey in a mighty bear hug. When Morrissey was nearly unconscious, a group of men barged into the ring, and they stopped the murder attempt.

A few months later, Poole was shot and killed by Morrissey's close friend Lew Baker at Stanwix Hall, a bar on Broadway near Prince Street. Both Baker and Morrissey were arrested for Poole's murder, but after three mistrials (rumor had it that Tammany Hall influenced some jurors in Morrissey and Baker's favor), the charges were finally dropped.

In 1857, Morrissey retired from boxing, and he went full-throttle into the gambling business. Morrissey eventually opened 16 gambling houses throughout the state of New York, including an exceptionally profitable one in Sarasota Springs.

From 1867-71, and with the backing of Tammany Hall, Morrissey was elected United States Congressman from New York. In 1873, tired of Tammany Hall's illegal tactics, which were only surpassed by the illegal tactics Morrissey employed himself, Morrissey testified against Tammany Hall chief and thief, William

"Boss" Tweed. Based on Morrissey's testimony and the overwhelming evidence of Tweed's treachery, the jury convicted Tweed on several counts of misappropriating government funds. As a result, Boss Tweed was sent to prison, where he subsequently died.

In 1875, as a reward for his service to his country, Morrissey was elected to the New York State Senate. Morrissey was still a Senator, when he died of pneumonia in 1878 at the age of 47.

In 1999, John Morrissey, A.K.A., "Old Smoke," was elected to the International Boxing Hall of Fame.

Timothy "Big Tim" Sullivan - 1894-1912

"Big Tim" Sullivan was a Tammany Hall hack who gave true meaning to the term "crooked politician."

Sullivan was born in 1863 at 25 Baxter Street, one of the worse slum buildings in New York City. At 25 Baxter Street, the squalor was so intense, in 1866, a *New York Times* article called it, "one of the filthiest tenements in New York City."

Sullivan's parents had emigrated from County Kerry, Ireland, and with them being so poor, Sullivan was thrust into the streets at the age of eight, to shine shoes and sell newspapers. Being the enterprising lad that he was, Sullivan soon saved up enough cash to start his own newspaper delivery service, in which Sullivan employed dozens of poor kids from the neighborhood to do his deliveries. In a few short years, Sullivan had enough cash to purchase four local bars; the first of which he opened on Christie Street, just east of the Bowery.

One of Sullivan's bar customers was Thomas "Fatty" Walsh, a notorious ward leader in Tammany Hall. Sullivan fell under Walsh's political wing, and in 1894, Sullivan was elected to the Third District's State Assembly.

Running roughshod over the rules, Sullivan became a large cog in Tammany Hall's corrupt wheel. Soon, Sullivan was appointed the District Leader of the entire Lower East Side of Manhattan.

That was like giving a vampire the key to the blood bank.

Sullivan bridged the gap between public service and common street thuggery, by recruiting infamous gang leaders, like Paul Kelly and Monk Eastman, to do his dirty work. This work included "voter influence" at election sites, which basically meant their gangs beat up voters who didn't see things exactly Sullivan's way.

In return for using his influence to keep these gangsters out of jail, Sullivan got a piece of all their illegal activities in the Lower East Side, including prostitution, gambling, loan-sharking, and extortion. To keep things looking on the up-and-up, Sullivan also entrenched himself in many legal endeavors, including becoming partners in the MGM and Loews cinema operations.

In Congress, Sullivan did pioneer a couple of key pieces of

legislation. In 1896, Sullivan introduced a law that made boxing legal, only to see it made illegal again in 1900 after several boxers were killed in the ring.

In 1911, Sullivan also passed the dubious "Sullivan Act" which made it illegal to carry guns, unless you could afford to pay a hefty registration fee. Needless to say, Sullivan's cronies made so much illegal dough, they all were able to cough up the cash needed to carry guns legally, in order to enforce their illegal activities. Yet, the common schmo on the street was so poor, he had no choice but to walk the mean streets of New York City without a firearm to protect himself.

In late 1911, Sullivan's evil ways finally caught up with him. Sullivan contracted syphilis, probably in one of the many prostitution houses in which he was a partner. As a result of this disease, Sullivan became paranoid and delusional. Sullivan was judged mentally incompetent, and he was removed from his seat in the Senate. In 1912, Sullivan's family placed him in a mental institution, which made his condition worse. While in the sanitarium, Sullivan complained he was being watched and that his food was being poisoned.

In 1913, while the guards were playing cards, Sullivan escaped from the sanitarium. Two weeks later, Sullivan's body was found near the railroad tracks in Pelham Parkway. It appeared, he had been hit by a freight train.

For some unknown reason, Sullivan's body was not claimed until 13 days later. The city declared him a vagrant, to be shamefully interred in a potter's field at Hart Island. As Sullivan's body was being readied for transport to Hart Island, a police officer made a final inspection of the corpse. He was astounded to discover that the dead man was, indeed, the missing Big Tim Sullivan. As a result, Big Tim was finally given a proper send-off.

After a jam-packed funeral ceremony at Old St. Patrick's Cathedral on Mulberry Street, an estimated 25,000 people lined the streets, as Sullivan's funeral reception made its way along Lower Manhattan and over the Williamsburg Bridge.

Sullivan was finally laid to rest at Calvary Cemetery in Long Island.

James Hines - The Ultimate Political Fixer 1907-1938

He started off as a simple Harlem blacksmith, but after he dug his
fat fingers deep into Tammany Hall, James Hines became the
biggest political fixer in the history of New York City.

Hines was born on December 18, 1876, on the Upper West Side
of Manhattan. His father operated a blacksmith shop on 121st Street
and Eight Avenue, and when his father became ill, Hines took over
his father's business at the age of 17.

Through his father's connections in politics in the 11th Assembly
District on the Upper West Side, Hines became close to "Big Tim"
Sullivan, a politician so crooked, he actually took part of the profits
from the rackets perpetrated by street gangs who were plundering the
Lower East Side of Manhattan. Sullivan was the main cog in the
political machine called Tammany Hall, and he played his
constituents like a fiddle, getting hand-picked people to vote several
times on Election Day by constantly changing their appearance.

Hines learned the ropes from the master, and in 1907 Hines ran
for a position called Alderman. With the help of Sullivan's
manipulation of the election process, Hines won the election going
away. (Sullivan had men, who wouldn't vote his way at the polls,
beaten up badly by his street gangs, most notable the Whyos.)

In 1910, Hines took the bold move of running for District
Leader against the incumbent. After both sides used roughhouse
tactics against the other, Hines was able to emerge victorious. With
his newfound power as District Leader, Hines formed the
Monongahela Democratic Club, which was his base of operations for
many years to come. At the Monongahela, Hines played the good
old boy; providing the poor in the neighborhood with Thanksgiving
turkeys, donating clothes to the needy and finding jobs for
whomever needed a job. Of course, that meant Hines could count on
those people's votes on Election Day for whomever candidate Hines
deemed should be the winner, no matter what district that candidate
was running in.

Every year, Hines sponsored the annual "June Walk and Picnic"
in Central Park, which drew as many 25,000 people, mostly children.
On one such occasion (The 22nd annual walk), Hines carried a kid on
piggyback, and then deposited him by a table brimming with a huge

spread of the finest food available.

Hines wiped the sweat from his brow, and said, "Kids who came to the first of these things are voters now. They're not all voting in my district, but they're voting somewhere. In politics, the thing to do is build yourself an army."

To supplement his income, and with no experience at all, Hines, along with his brother, Philip, formed a trucking company and then a construction company. Almost immediately, the Hines brothers were able to obtain the best and the biggest city trucking contracts and state construction projects, which they subsequently subcontracted out to people who actually knew how to do those jobs.

Even though Hines was the biggest player of his time in Democratic politics, he had very little future in running for elective office. Hines was an unskilled public speaker and was more adept at back room dealings, where a mere nod of his head would signify which person was getting elected, or appointed to a political job. As generous as he could be with his friends, if someone crossed Hines, as far Hines was concerned, that person may as well have been dead.

During Prohibition, Owney "The Killer" Madden and "Big Bill" Dwyer were running the biggest bootlegging and rum running operations in the entire United States of America. However, both men knew their business could never thrive if they didn't have the police in their back pockets. And the man who controlled the all police promotions at the time was none other than Jim Hines. Dwyer and Madden paid Hines, and they paid him well, to take care of the police, judges, prosecutors, and bail bondsmen. By taking care of Hines properly, Madden and Dwyer knew if any of their men did have the misfortune of being arrested by a cop, who either wasn't getting paid, or was just being plain disobedient, Hines would arrange for that person's immediate release.

Tammany big shot George Washington Plunkitt, a man who schooled Hines when Hines first started out in politics, said that is was a good idea for a crooked politician like Hines to be associated with known gangsters. Plunkitt believed, and with good reason, that if anyone was considering either to report Hines to the authorities, or to refuse Hines's demands, they'd think twice, knowing someone like Owney "The Killer" Madden was waiting in the wings to correct them if they did.

Plunkitt once explained exactly what a District Leader like

Hines was expected to do.

He said, "As a rule a District Leader has no business or occupation other than politics. He plays politics every day and night of the year and his headquarters bears the inscription 'Never Closed.'"

Madden and Dwyer met often with Hines at his Monongahela Democratic Club on the Upper West Side to discuss business. Some of this business concerned which politician was the best for the business of the "Combine," as Madden and Dwyer's operation was called. In 1925, it was decided by all that ex-Tin Pan Alley songwriter Jimmy Walker would be the perfect pick for New York City Mayor. With Hines's backing and Madden's control of the polling places, Walker won the election by a landslide.

In 1929, Walker was reelected, this time defeating reformer and future mayor Fiorello LaGuardia. But Walker was as crooked as they came, and he spent very little time actually being mayor of New York City.

Once, after he was questioned by a political opponent after he gave himself a raise from $25,000 to $40,000 a year, Walker quipped, "Hell, that's cheap. Imagine what I would be worth if I worked full time."

But all good things must come to an end. In 1932, after Walker was grilled by the Seabury Committee, which was looking into police and political corruption, New York Governor Franklin D. Roosevelt, working hand-in-hand with Hines, pressured Walker to resign. Walker, taking the cue, quit his office immediately. Accompanied by his girlfriend Betty Compton, Walker jumped on the first boat available, and they traveled to the friendly confines of France. Walker remained in France for four years, before he deemed it safe to return to New York City.

The Presidential election of 1932 was an even bigger coup for Hines. In 1928, New York Governor Al Smith, a man who had tried to take control of Tammany Hall from Hines, ran unsuccessfully for the President of the United States against Republican Herbert Hoover. Under Hoover, the stock market crashed in 1929, and by 1932, America was in the throes of The Great Depression. Smith wanted to run for President again, but he was opposed by Roosevelt, who had taken Smith's place as Governor in 1928.

Hines had a long memory concerning Smith, and he threw all

his weight behind Roosevelt for the Democratic nomination for President. Roosevelt won the Democratic nomination against Smith quite easily and also the Presidential election against Herbert Hoover. With his man Roosevelt snug in the White House, Roosevelt rewarded Hines for his unyielding service by giving Hines the job of awarding all federal patronage in Manhattan to whomever Hines deemed fit for the jobs.

By 1933, Hines was riding high in New York City politics. Tainted money was flowing into his coffers from the mobsters, and Hines was known as a "King Maker," a man who could influence any election he chose to, throughout New York State, and if need be, anywhere in America.

The start of Hines's downfall was when Hines was introduced by his fellow gangsters to the only gangster in New York City whom Hines wasn't doing favors for: Dutch Schultz (real name Arthur Flegenheimer). The first meeting was so secretive, it started with Hines waiting surreptitiously under the elevated trains on a street corner on Sixth Avenue in Greenwich Village, far away from Hines's domain on the Upper West Side. Minutes later, Schultz picked up Hines in a bulletproof Cadillac. Also in the Caddy was Schultz's associate George Weinberg and Schultz's lawyer and master fixer, Dixie Davis.

In 1938, when Hines was a defendant in the first of his two trials for political corruption, George Weinberg testified in court for the prosecution. Weinberg spoke in great detail about the pivotal conversation which took place in the Cadillac amongst himself, Hines, and Schultz, on that fateful day in 1933.

Weinberg said, "I explained to Hines, that in order to be able to run our business and bring it up the right way, we would have to protect the controllers that are working for us. We would have to protect them from going to jail, and if we got any big arrests that would hurt our business, we would want them dismissed in Magistrates' Court, so that they wouldn't have to go downtown (Weinberg was referring to the tougher three-judge Court of Special Sessions). I explained to him that we did not mind the small arrests, but if we got any large arrests we would want them dismissed in Magistrates' Court, to show the people in Harlem who are working for us that we had the right kind of protection up there, and that we would want to protect them from going to jail."

In the bulletproof Caddy, Hines and Schultz came to an agreement that Schultz would give Hines, as a measure of his good will, one thousand dollars on the spot. Also, Schultz told Hines that Dixie Davis would be the go-between to funnel Hines another $500 per week, to keep Schultz's various enterprises free from law enforcement intervention.

In 1937, when Davis himself was tried for policy rackets involvement, he testified in court, "I cultivated Jimmy Hines right from the beginning. I soon learned that to run an organized mob you've got to have a politician. You have heard about the suspected link between organized crime and politics. Well, I became the missing link."

Davis also testified that Schultz's policy banks kicked in the $500 a week for Hines, but that Davis, "tossed in another $500 himself to Hines without even telling Schultz." Davis said that he put up the extra money, so that the big spender (Hines) had the cash he needed for the "Friday Night Fights, and whatever else Hines needed to do when Mr. Hines did the necessary entertaining - judges, officeholders, big businessmen - that kept his political power mower oiled."

Because of his cooperation, Davis was sentenced to a mere one year in prison, plus he was disbarred.

Hines also controlled the appointments of the various New York judges. And when he did appoint a judge, Hines made it clear that the judge now worked for him and was compelled to do anything Hines said needed to be done.

On one occasion, Weinberg and his boys were caught with the goods, when an enterprising detective busted into an apartment they used for business. Once inside, the bull was pleased to discover the apartment contained over $20,000 worth of policy racket receipts. Weinberg told the detective that he was making a very big mistake, and if he insisted on arresting Weinberg and his men, the detective would soon be busted back to uniformed cop, walking a beat somewhere in Harlem.

After he was released on bail, Weinberg immediately ran to Hines. After hearing Weinberg's story, Hines told Weinberg he would take care of the situation.

That same night, Hines took Weinberg to a steak dinner at the Andrew B. Keating Democratic Club, where they met a Hines appointee, the very honorable (not) Judge Hulon Capshaw.

Hines told the judge, "I have a policy case, a very important one, coming up before you that I'd like you to take care of for me."

The judge replied, "I haven't failed you yet. I'll take care of it."

And that the judge did, when he ruled that the policy slips found in the apartment could in no way be connected to the men who were in that same apartment. The case was dismissed, and the detective who did the aborted bust was soon busted himself, back to patrolman, by Police Commissioner James Bolan, also a Hines appointee.

The wheels started spinning off Hines's gravy train when Special Prosecutor Thomas E. Dewey began investigating Dutch Schultz's voluminous illegal business activities. The Dutchman didn't like the heat too much, so he told the other men on the National Crime Commission, of which he was a member with gangsters like Lucky Luciano, Meyer Lansky, Bugsy Siegel, and Frank Costello, that he wanted Dewey hit and hit right away.

When the Commission voted down his request, Schultz said, "I still say Dewey should be hit, and I'm going to do it myself."

The Commission didn't like hearing that too much, so on October 23, 1935, to save Dewey's life, Schultz was shot in the bathroom of the Palace Chophouse at 12 East Park Street in Newark, New Jersey. Schultz lingered for a few hours at the hospital, in a delirious state, before he finally stopped breathing for good.

With Schultz now eliminated, Dewey turned his attention to Hines. Dewey claimed that Hines was "a co-conspirator and indispensable functionary of the Schultz organization."

Things started looking mighty bad for Hines, when George Weinberg suddenly turned canary and testified against Hines at Hines's first trial in 1938. With Weinberg talking non-stop on the witness stand about Hines's involvement in Schultz's rackets, Hines seemed doomed to be convicted. However, on September 12, 1938, four days into the trial, a mistrial was declared on a technicality, by New York General Sessions Court Justice Pecora.

As Hines was waiting to be re-tried by Dewey, George Weinberg suddenly became overcome with grief for turning rat against Hines. Down and depressed, Weinberg fired a fatal bullet into his own brain.

With Weinberg out of the picture, it looked like Hines was in the clear. However, Hines took a roundhouse right to the jaw, when the new judge ruled in Hines's second trail (which took place in 1939), that Weinberg's testimony from the first trial could be admitted into evidence.

With corroborating testimony from men like Police Commissioner James Bolan and crooked Tammany Hall politician John Curry, Hines was found guilty on all thirteen counts of the indictment; one of which was accepting more than $200,000 in bribes from Dutch Schultz.

As Hines left the courthouse, he was asked by a snotty reporter if Hines felt "tired."

Hines snapped back, "How would you feel if you were just kicked in the belly?"

As a result of his convictions, Hines was sentenced to 4-8 years in prison. But he was released on parole on September 12, 1944, after serving a little more than five years of his bit.

Living alone with his wife in their home on a beach in Long Island, Hines spent the rest of his years in relative obscurity. On March 26, 1957, James "The King Maker" Hines died of natural causes at the age of 80.

Jimmy Walker– New York City's "Midnight Mayor" – 1924-1932

If New York City Mayor Jimmy Walker had not been so likable he would certainly have been branded a scoundrel.

Jimmy Walker was born in New York City's Greenwich Village on June 19, 1881, the son of an Irish immigrant, who later became a political mover and shaker in Tammany Hall. Walker attended Xavier High School, which is a military school in Manhattan, and later New York Law School.

However, Walker's first love was music. Walker fell in with the Village's bohemian crowd, and instead of practicing law, he turned to songwriting. Two of the songs Walker wrote were: *There's Music In The Rustle Of A Skirt* and *Will You Love Me in December As You Do in May?* The latter song made Walker an overnight sensation in Tin Pan Alley, with its melodious refrain:

Will you love me in December as you do in May?
Will you love in the good old fashioned way?
When my hair has all turned Gray,
Will you kiss me then, and say,
That you love me in December as you do in May?

In 1910, due to his father's prodding, and with the influence of his mentor, Tammany Hall titan Al Smith (later Governor Smith), Walker ran and was elected to the New York State Assembly, where he served until 1914. Savoring the taste of political power, the now-ambitious Walker was then elected to the New York State Senate from 1914 to 1925. Walker was so popular in the Senate, he was elected President pro tempore of the New York State Senate from 1923 to 1924.

Throughout his term in the Senate, Walker was always smartly dressed, and he was imbued with a radiant, outgoing attitude. Walker was considered a bon vivant, who spent more time bending his elbow in speakeasies than he did actually serving his constituents in the Senate.

American journalist Robert Caro once described Senator Walker as, "Pinch-waisted, one-button suit, slenderest of cravats, a shirt from a collection of hundreds, pearl-gray spats buttoned around silk-hosed ankles, toes of the toothpick shoes peeking out from the spats polished to a gleam. Pixie smile, the 'vivacity of a song and dance man,' a charm that made him arrive in the Senate Chamber like a glad breeze. 'The Prince Charming of Politics'.....slicing through the ponderous arguments of the ponderous men who sat around him with a wit that flashed like a rapier. Beau James."

In 1925, Al Smith, then Governor of New York, thought Walker would be the perfect mayor for New York City, a town now basking in the glow of the naughtiness of the Roaring 20's. With Smith's backing and backroom maneuvering, Walker moved to unseat the present mayor John Harlan, who was considered quite competent if not a bit stodgy.

Smith's biggest roadblock was that Walker was known more as a party animal than he was as a wily politician. But "Beau James," as he was now called in the press, promised Smith, if he was elected to the top spot in town, he would mend his wayward ways.

Harlan was a Democrat, and so was Walker, so Smith had to call in some of his outstanding chits in order for Walker to get the Democratic nomination. That mission accomplished, Walker's next obstacle was Republican-Fusion candidate Frank Waterman in the mayoral election.

Waterman basically called Walker a crook, and said that if Walker were elected mayor, because of Walker's crooked ties in Tammany Hall, the New York City Subway system would be immersed in corruption. Walker laughed off Waterman's remarks, and he said he was running as the "people's mayor," because he liked to do the same things the general public liked to do: gambling and drinking illegal hooch during Prohibition.

During his campaign, Walker boasted, "I like the company of my fellow human beings. I like the theater and am devoted to healthy outdoor sports. Because I like these things, I have reflected my attitude in some of my legislation I have sponsored: 2.75 percent beer, Sunday baseball, Sunday movies, and legalized boxing. But let me allay any fear there may be that, because I believe in personal liberty, wholesome amusement, and healthy professional sport, I will not countenance for a moment any indecency or vice in New York."

Yeah, right.

In a blur, Walker partied his way through his first four years as mayor. The public was so in love with the new mayor, it hardly caused a ripple when he left his wife, Janet, for showgirl Betty Compton, who was 23 years Walker's junior.

In 1928, Walker's shenanigans lost him the favor of Al Smith. So Walker, the cool cat that he was, cozied up to the new governor, Franklin D. Roosevelt, who had been elected governor when Smith stepped down to run for the Presidency against Republican Herbert Hoover. After losing to Hoover, Smith's power at Tammany Hall was greatly diminished. Roosevelt was the new Democratic power in New York State, and the wily Walker took advantage of that.

That's not to say Walker accomplished nothing in his first term as mayor. Walker did consolidate the New York City hospital system, purchased thousands of acres for park land (including Great Kills in Staten Island), and he expanded the municipal bus system. The fact that a few of his pals were granted an exclusive franchise to own the city buses caused not a ripple in Walker's popularity. In fact, no one said a word that Walker had basically become a part-time mayor.

"Beau James" was hardly ever in City Hall attending to business, and was instead either at the racetrack, the fights, or carousing in one of the city's 32,000 speakeasies. While enjoying the nightlife, Walker imbibed his share of illegal beverages. Walker's favorite cocktail was a "Black Velvet," which is champagne poured over the top of a hefty serving of Guinness stout.

In 1929, Walker was challenged for mayor by the fiery reformer, Fiorello LaGuardia. During one heated debate, LaGuardia was incensed that Walker had raised his own salary from $25,000 a year to $40,000 a year. Walked quipped back, "Hell, that's cheap. Imagine what I would be worth if I worked full time."

Walker chided LaGuardia's reputation as a "reformer," saying, "Reformers are guys who ride through a sewer in a glass bottom boat." Meaning, a savvy politician knew well enough to look the other way when it was politically expedient to do so.

Walker didn't know it at the time, but the beginning of his undoing was the stock-market crash of 1929. It was all right to act carefree and gay when the city was enjoying economic growth, but when people were out of work, with some even starving, Walker's devil-may-care attitude began to wear thin.

Walker faced his first real embarrassment, in July of 1930, when he and his gal-pal, Betty Compton, were present when the police raided a gambling house in Montauk, Long Island.

While people were being lined up against the wall and handcuffed, Walker told the local police something like, "Hey, I'm the mayor of New York City! You can't arrest the mayor of New York City!"

The police agreed, and they let Walker go. But being "The girlfriend of the mayor of New York City" had no such pull. So the cops cuffed Compton and led her to the local slammer. It took Walker a few hours to reach the right people to get Compton released.

Still, since the embarrassing incident was reported in the press, it left a big scar on Walker's reputation, because it was evident, while people were starving and out of work and sometimes denied food and shelter, "Beau James" was having a grand old time for himself. And let the city of New York be damned.

Things started to turn bleak for Walker when the Archbishop of New York, Cardinal Hayes, started taking pot shots at the mayor. Hayes claimed that the decadence of New York City, which led to the stock-market crash of 1929, was mostly the fault of Mayor Walker, whose shady antics set a bad example for the rest of the city. Cardinal Hayes even accused Walker of looking the other way while girlie magazines were being sold by the thousands on 42nd Street.

Walker foolishly took on Cardinal Hayes, when he fired back, "I never knew a woman who was hurt by a magazine."

Cardinal Hayes kept up his attacks on Walker, and soon the cardinal's rants reached the office of Roosevelt, who was readying himself to run for President of the United States. As a result, Roosevelt was not too happy with Mayor Walker, and he was looking for a way to rid himself of Walker's political embarrassments.

Walker had one foot in his political grave and another foot on a banana peel, when he was summoned before the Seabury Committee, chaired by Justice Samuel Seabury, a cantankerous man obviously disgusted by Mayor Walker's excesses. The Seabury Committee was formed to investigate police and political corruption in New York City.

On May 25, 1932, Walker, dressed like he was going speakeasy-hopping, mounted the steps of the county courthouse in lower

Manhattan.

A throng of well-wishers clapped at his arrival, yelling, "Atta boy, Jimmy! You tell 'em Jimmy! Good luck boyo!"

Walker flashed his million-dollar smile, and he raised his clasped hands over his head like a professional boxer after winning a fight.

Then Mayor Walker entered the lion's den and came face to face with Justice Seabury.

Right off the bat, there was terrible tension between the two men, who couldn't be more different in personality and in demeanor. Over a two-day period, Seabury spat his questions at Walker, and Walker fired back with the utmost contempt.

At one point Walker yelled at Seabury, "You and Franklin Roosevelt are not going to hoist yourself to the Presidency over my dead body."

While Seabury hammered hard questions at Walker, it became evident that "Beau James" had insulated himself from direct connection to any political skullduggery. However, it was highly embarrassing to Walker, when it was discovered that there had been cash payments made to his girlfriend Betty Compton after some connected businesses were awarded lucrative contracts from the powers-that-be in New York City; which included Walker,

In addition, Walker's brother Dr. William H. Walker, who had a monopoly on worker's compensation claims, seemed to have banked over $500,000 in a four-year period. Seabury uncovered evidence that William Walker had, in fact, padded many of the workman's comp claims and had secreted the difference into his own coffers.

Even though Seabury could not pin one illegal act on Mayor Walker himself, it was obvious that Walker had been blasted with political blows he could never recover from. As a result of the Seabury investigation, Seabury penned a recommendation to Governor Roosevelt which said that Walker should be removed from office for "gross improprieties and other instances of political malfeasance."

Governor Roosevelt was just months away from the presidential elections. And since Walker still had legions of supporters in New York City, Roosevelt wasn't sure what was the best way to handle the Walker situation.

Walker took Roosevelt off the hook, when on September 1,

1932, he announced his resignation as Mayor of New York City.

Within days, Walker hopped on a cruise ship to Europe, accompanied by his showgirl girlfriend, Betty Compton. In 1933, Walker divorced his wife and married Compton. For three years, Walker spent his self-imposed exile in London with Compton. When Walker returned to New York City, LaGuardia was mayor, and Walker was out of politics for good.

Shunned by the political arena, Walker returned to his first love: the music industry. Walker became head of Majestic Records, a big-band record label that included such popular musicians as Louie Prima and Bud Freeman. In 1946, two years after he assumed control of Majestic Records, Walker died of a brain hemorrhage at the age of 65. Walker was buried in the Gates of Heaven Cemetery in Hawthorne, New York.

In 1957, comedian and song-and-dance-man Bob Hope starred in a movie based on Walker's life called *Beau James*. This film was based on a biography of Walker, also titled *Beau James*, written by Gene Fowler. This book was also used as the basis for *Jimmy*, a Broadway play about Walker, that ran from October 1969 to January 1970. In *Jimmy*, Frank Gorshin played Walker and Anita Gillette played Betty Compton.

In the 1959 Broadway musical *Fiorello!*, the song *Gentleman Jimmy*, was dedicated to New York City's "Midnight Mayor," Jimmy Walker.

Thomas E. Dewey– The Special Prosecutor from Hell - 1931-1938

He was a mean-spirited runt; a little man with a large mustache that seemed to dominate his snarling face. However, liberal Republican Thomas E. Dewey, a man who made his bones as a Special Prosecutor in New York City and who would stop at nothing to further his skyrocketing career, was just an eyelash away from becoming President of the United States.

Dewey was born on March 24, 1902 in the little town of Owosso, Mich. Dewey's father was the editor and publisher of the local newspaper: the *Owosso Times*. Dewey Senior's mission in life was to right the wrongs of the political world, especially the tyranny of Tammany Hall, a corrupt Democratic political machine based in New York City, but with tentacles that reached all around America. Dewey Junior admired his father's zeal, and this later motivated Dewey to go after organized crime figures in New York City with a vengeance that not always adhered to the letter of the law.

But first Dewey wanted to sing.

Dewey was a talented operatic baritone, and while he was attending the University of Michigan he joined the Phi Mu Alpha Sinfonia, a national fraternity for men of music. Dewey was also a member of the University of Michigan Men's Glee Club. Following in his father's footsteps, Dewey wrote for *The Michigan Daily*, the university's student newspaper. However, Dewey was better at singing than he was at writing, so much so, that in 1923, Dewey finished third in the National Singing Contest. However, Dewey soon developed throat problems, and although he briefly considered a career in music, he opted to become a lawyer instead.

With his father's money, Dewey traveled to New York City, and he enrolled at the Columbia Law School. One of his classmates was the radical socialist/communist Paul Robeson, who became a singer and actor of some note, in between moving to and from the country he really loved: Russia.

However, Dewey was no idealist like Robeson. After he graduated law school in just two years, Dewey decided to hang up his own shingle and go into private practice, which he did from 1925-31. In 1928, Dewey married actress Frances Hutt. After their marriage, Dewey's wife quit acting, and they eventually raised two sons: Thomas E. Dewey Jr., and John Martin Dewey.

In 1931, Dewey was named chief assistant to George Medalie and was given the official title of Chief Assistant U.S. Attorney for the Southern District of New York. This was the springboard Dewey needed to further a political career which knew no boundaries and counted heavily on legal improprieties.

In 1933, Dewey's first major case was the prosecution of former pickpocket Irving Wexler, better known as Waxey Gordon. Gordon was a protégé of Arnold Rothstein, considered "The Godfather" of the modern gangster. In 1928, after Rothstein was killed over a large gambling debt, Gordon took over Rothstein's operations, in bootlegging and in the gambling business. Gordon's partners in crime included such illustrious gangsters like Lucky Luciano, Louis "Lepke" Buchalter, Gurrah Shapiro, and Meyer Lansky. Even after cutting in his partners, Gordon was said to have made over $2 million a year in profits.

However, Gordon and Lansky hated each other, and after Dewey unsuccessfully tried to prosecute Gordon for his crimes, Lansky, with the blessing of Luciano and Buchalter, funneled information, including specific documentation, to Dewey that showed that maybe Gordon was not paying his fair share of his income taxes.

Using the same tactic the government had utilized against Al Capone, Dewey, now in the possession of books that said Gordon had hidden $5 million in taxable income over a 10-year period, lowered the boom on Gordon. Dewey cross-examined Gordon with such cruelty, spit was proverbially flying from Dewey's mouth and down his copious mustache.

Gordon, basically an oaf with the mentally and vocabulary of a 10-year-old, was no match for Dewey on the witness stand. After the most one-sided trial that could possibly occur, Gordon was slapped with a 10-year prison sentence.

Dewey next set his sights on Dutch Schultz.

By the time Dewey was ready to prosecute Schultz, it was alleged that District Attorney William C. Dodge was not aggressively going after the mob and crooked politicians, and in New York City there were plenty of both. In 1935, Dewey got a bump up in rank, when Governor Herbert H. Lehman, bypassing

Dodge, appointed Dewey as Special Prosecutor in New York County (Manhattan). With the backing of Governor Lehman, Dewey assembled a crack staff of more than 60 assistants, investigators, process servers, stenographers, and clerks. New York Mayor Fiorello H. La Guardia contributed 63 of his best police officers to the cause, and Dewey was on top of the prosecutorial world.

Dutch Schultz, born Arthur Flegenheimer on August 6, 1902, was the most visible mobster in New York City. However, Schultz was only one of a nine-member National Crime Commission which included Italians gangsters Lucky Luciano and Frank Costello, as well as fellow Jewish mobsters Meyer Lansky, Bugsy Siegel, and Louis "Lepke" Buchalter.

During Prohibition, Schultz made millions in the sale of illegal beer and was nicknamed "The Beer Baron of the Bronx." In the early 1920s, Schultz bulldozed his way into the Harlem numbers rackets, pushing aside notable black number kings Madame Stephanie St. Clair, Bumpy Johnson, and Casper Holstein.

Noted crime author and former cop Ralph Salerno once said, "Schultz asked the black numbers to a meeting in his office. When they came in, Schultz put his forty-five on the desk and said, 'I'm your partner.'"

Holstein backed off quietly, but St. Clair and her muscle Johnson, decided to fight back against Schultz. Johnson went as far as to visit Lucky Luciano downtown in Little Italy to plead his case. Luciano admired the spunk of Johnson, but he told Johnson that Schultz was his partner in other endeavors and that he had to back his partner. Luciano advised Johnson to tell St. Clair it was in their best interest to work under Schultz in the Harlem numbers game. St. Clair refused at first, but after the word was put out on the Harlem streets that St. Clair was to be shot on sight, she agreed to Luciano's proposition.

Schultz also made a ton of cash taking illegal bets on sporting events. Schultz owned the Coney Island racetrack in Cincinnati, Ohio, where the daily three-digit Harlem number was derived from the last three digits of the total mutual handle for that day. Schultz was able to manipulate those daily numbers by having his numbers wiz, Otto "Abbadabba" Berman, determine which three-digit numbers were bet heavily that day. Then Berman would call the track before the last race to change the last three digits to numbers which were bet lightly, or maybe not at all. Schultz also had a vast array of illegal slot machines placed all over New York City, which pumped out cash like water gushing down Niagara Falls.

As much money as he had accumulated, Schultz dressed like a broken-down valise.

Luciano once said of Schultz, "He has all the money in the world, but he dresses like a bum."

Schultz claimed he never spent more than two dollars for a shirt in his life.

"Only queers wear silk shirts," Schultz said.

The Feds had their first shot at Schultz, when they indicted him for income tax evasion. But the wily Schultz went into the wind for several months, and when he did turn himself in, his lawyer was somehow able to move the trial venue to the sleepy upstate town of Malone, New York.

Schultz went to Malone months before the trial, and he contributed money to local causes like he was the Salvation Army. Schultz, a non-practicing Jew, even converted to Catholicism in order to garner the support of the Malone locals, who were overwhelmingly Catholic.

The trial was a slam dunk for Schultz, and he walked out of the Malone courtroom with a loopy smile on his face, as a free man.

However, a prosecution captained by the mighty Dewey was a different proposition for Schultz.

When Schultz got word that Dewey had him in his crosshairs, Schultz called for an emergency meeting of the nine-man National Crime Commission.

At this meeting Schultz said, "Dewey will not stop until all of us Commission members are in jail." Schultz then slammed his hand on the table for emphasis, "We have to take Dewey out!"

The other commission members were skeptical of Schultz's demands. But they decided to table Schultz's request to see how easy it might be gunning down Dewey. They gave the chore to Albert Anastasia, a ruthless killer, and one of the bosses of Murder Incorporated. Anastasia was known on the streets as the "Lord High Executioner."

In order to clock Dewey's movements, Anastasia borrowed a baby from a friend for several days. Anastasia pushed the baby in a carriage around 214 Fifth Avenue, the posh apartment building where Dewey lived. As Anastasia strolled the streets pushing the baby carriage, he was able to ascertain Dewey's exact weekday morning movements.

Dewey exited the apartment building at 8 a.m. sharp every weekday morning. Surrounded by a phalanx of bodyguards, Dewey would walk a few blocks to a neighborhood drug store for his morning coffee and to make a phone call from a pay phone in the back. While Dewey was alone in the back of the drug store, his men stood guard like mastiffs out front.

Anastasia figured he could be waiting at the counter when Dewey entered, and then kill Dewey before Dewey could reach the pay phone in the back. Other Murder Incorporated killers would take care of Dewey's bodyguards in front of the drug store.

The following week, after Schultz was asked to leave the room, Anastasia presented his plan to the rest of the Commission. Even though the deed could possibly be done, it was decided that if they did kill Dewey, all hell would break loose on their rackets. The only one, besides Schultz, who voted for the hit was Gurrah Shapiro.

Manhattan D.A. Frank Hogan later said, "I suppose they figured the National Guard would have been called out if Dewey was killed. And I guess they wouldn't have been far wrong."

When Schultz was called back into the room and told the bad news, he exploded into a rage. "Dewey's got to go!" Schultz said. "I'm hitting him myself within 48 hours."

This did not please the rest of the Commission members too much. They immediately decided that Schultz, for the greater good of the Commission, was the one who had to go.

Luciano and Lansky figured that since Schultz was Jewish, Jewish gangsters were the proper choice in ending the life of a Jewish mob boss. Lansky decided to use two of Murder Incorporated's best men: Charlie "The Bug" Workman and Mendy Weiss. The place for the hit was set to be Schultz's hangout: The Palace Chop House in Newark, New Jersey. A nobody named Piggy, who was familiar with the Newark streets, was selected as the getaway driver.

On October 23, 1935, at approximately 10:15 p.m., Piggy parked a dark sedan outside The Palace Chop House. Workman and Weiss exited the car, guns drawn. They entered the restaurant and found the front room empty, but there was lively chatter coming from the back room. When the killers entered the back room, they spotted Schultz's top men, Lulu Rosenkrantz, Abe Landau, and Abbadabba Berman finishing the remains of their last supper.

With blazing guns in both hands, Workman and Weiss opened fire. Landau and Rosenkrantz returned fire after they were hit, but they were turned into Swiss cheese and rendered quite dead.

"It was like a Wild West Show," Workman said later.

However, Dutch Schultz was nowhere to be found.

After Workman emptied his .38, he dropped it to the floor, and then he rushed, holding his .45, into the bathroom where he found Schultz in a stall. Workman fired the .45 twice. Schultz ducked the first slug, but the second slug found its mark just below his chest. The bullet blasted through Schultz's stomach, large intestine, gall bladder, and liver, before falling on the floor next to him.

Schultz was rushed to the hospital, and he was in the state of delirium, talking utter nonsense, until he passed away the following evening.

Before Schultz died, a telegram was delivered to his death bed. It read, "As ye reap, also shall ye sow."

It was signed "Madame St. Clair."

With Schultz out of the way, and Dewey still very much alive, Dewey turned his sights on the second-most visible mobster in New York City: Charles "Lucky" Luciano.

Luciano was a high-ranking member on the National Crime Commission, and he metaphorically spat in Dewey's face by showing up almost every night in swank nightclubs all around town with a knockout broad on each arm.

The problem was, Luciano, along with his close friend Meyer Lansky (who was a quiet homebody and didn't irk Dewey as much as Luciano did), were almost untouchable, because of the several layers of insulation they had placed between themselves and the crimes committed on the streets by their underlings. Plus, both Luciano and Lansky had several legitimate business interests, with savvy accountants, who made sure the proper amounts of taxes were paid to the government.

So what was Dewey to do? It was simple and diabolical all the same. Dewey decided to frame Luciano for one of the few crimes Luciano wasn't committing.

At the time, Luciano lived in a swank apartment (room 39D) at the Waldorf-Astoria, under the name of Mr. Ross. Dewey was cutting a wide swath through New York City; first going after the gambling rackets and then setting his sights on prostitution.

On January 31, 1936, Dewey ordered his men to raid more than 80 brothels, pick up every prostitute in sight (even ones walking the streets), arrest pimps of all colors and nationalities, and bring them one-by-one into his office in the Woolworth Building.

The broads were hardened hookers with colorful names like Sadie the Chink, Jennie the Factory, and Polack Francis. The pimps were low-level street hustlers who kicked up their money to mobsters, who in turn kicked it up the ladder, until some of it allegedly made its way into the hands of a "Mr. Ross."

All of the arrestees had one thing in common: they did not want to go to jail.

So even though Luciano detested prostitution and never had his fingers in its dirty pie, it was possible that some of the dough kicked up to him by his captains had originated in sex dens. All Dewey had to do was to prove it in a court of law, whichever way he could.

In mid-1936, spurred on by the testimony of hookers and pimps who had never even met Luciano, Dewey ordered a warrant for Luciano's arrest on the charge of running a huge prostitution ring. Luciano, outraged at being charged with something he had nothing to do with, dodged the warrant by traveling down to Hot Springs, Ark., to a resort run by his old pal Owney "The Killer" Madden. After making untold millions in the rum running and gambling enterprises, Madden had retired from the rackets, and re-invented himself in Hot Springs as a successful businessman and hotelier.

If it had been a gambling pinch, Luciano would have lawyered up with the best attorneys in town, turned himself in, and he would have stood a decent chance of beating the rap. But prostitution was uncharted territory for Luciano.

His pal Lansky would later say, "Charlie had the same revulsion about running brothels that I did. He believed no respectable man ever made money from a woman in that horrible way."

It took four months for Dewey to locate Luciano, and when he did, he sent 20 Arkansas Rangers to Madden's resort, where they cuffed Luciano and threw him on a train back to New York City.

It was a three-week trial, and Luciano never stood a chance.

Dewey paraded hooker after hooker, and pimp after pimp onto

the witness stand. The hookers told of the degradation they had suffered toiling in the field of their choice. And the pimps testified that the money the hookers handed over to them was kicked up the ladder to Mr. Ross – a.k.a. Lucky Luciano.

When Luciano took the stand, his coarse manner stood in stark contrast to the intelligent and erudite Dewey, who had been training for this moment all his life. When the verdict came in, Luciano was found guilty of 558 counts, and he was sentenced to 30-50 years in prison; the longest prison sentence ever rendered for prostitution in United States history.

There was immediate outrage in the ranks of organized crime throughout America. All the top gangsters knew for sure Luciano never had a thing to do with prostitution. Dewey had broken the rules, and he showed no shame in doing so.

In 1941, the imprisoned Gurrah Shapiro sent a note to his pal Louie Lepke, who was awaiting the electric chair.

The note said, "I told you we should have killed Dewey when we had the chance."

In Rich Cohen's book *Tough Jews,* Cohen said crime writer and former cop Ralph Salerno had once told him on this subject; "The gangsters said to us: Don't frame me. Don't drop a little envelope in my pocket, then run up and say 'I caught you with narcotics.' That's a frame-up. That's a no-no. That's what I demand of you, Ralph. But what I give you in return is, if you ever catch me right, I go to jail and do my time. And they don't drag me out of the courtroom saying, 'You son of a bitch, you and your family are dead.' None of that crap. I'm a professional. And if you be a professional too and catch me right, then it's not personal."

Luciano did a little over 10 years in the slammer. But after World War II, he was freed from jail. As part of his deal with the government for having his men protect the waterfront from enemy sabotage, Luciano was deported to Italy. One of the men who signed off on this deal was New York Governor Thomas E. Dewey. It was also alleged, in 1944 and again in 1948, when Dewey was running for President of the United States, Luciano's pals had contributed $600,000 to Dewey's campaign coffers.

In 1962, before he died of a heart attack at the Naples International Airport, Luciano wrote in his autobiography *The Last Testament*, which he planned to make into a movie, "After sittin' in court and listenin' to myself being plastered to the wall, and tarred and feathered by a bunch of whores who sold themselves for a quarter, and hearin' that no-good McCook [the judge] hand me what added to a life term, I still get madder at Dewey's crap than anythin' else. That little shit with the mustache comes right out in the open and admits he's got me on everythin' else but what he charged me with. I knew he knew I didn't have a fuckin' thing to do with prostitution, not with none of those broads. But Dewey was such a goddamn racketeer himself, in a legal way, that he crawled up my back with a frame and stabbed me."

With the Luciano trophy on his prosecutorial mantle, Dewey set his sights on one of Luciano's fellow National Crime commission members: Louis "Lepke" Buchalter. But Buchalter, still seething over the way Dewey railroaded Luciano, went on the lam for four years to avoid prosecution. When Lepke finally turned himself in 1939, Dewey already had bigger fish to fry: he decided he wanted to become governor of the state of New York.

In 1938, Edwin Jaeckle, the New York Republican Party Chairman, selected Dewey, only 36-years-old, to run for governor against the extremely popular incumbent governor Herbert H. Lehman. The liberal Republican Dewey ran his entire campaign on his record as "racket-buster," especially the successful prosecution (frame-up) of Lucky Luciano.

However, Lehman, on the coattails of his association with the popular President of the United States, Franklin D. Roosevelt, won a close election, beating Dewey by a mere 1.4 percent of the vote. But Dewey's good showing against Lehman propelled him into being one of the leaders of the Republican Party.

In 1940, Dewey tried to get the Republican nomination for President to run against FDR. Although he was considered an early favorite, most Republican bigwigs thought Dewey, then 38, was too young and inexperienced to go against a titan like FDR. With the threat of World War II imminent, the Republicans wanted a leader more experienced than Dewey to lead our nation in wartime. They instead selected Wendell Willkie to run for president. Willkie lost by a landslide to FDR, who won his third term as President.

In 1942, Dewey ran for governor of New York again. And this time he won by an avalanche over Democrat John J. Bennett. Dewey would run for governor twice more, in 1946 and 1950, and he would be successful both times. But Dewey's goal was the presidency, and when Dewey sunk his teeth into something, he never let go.

In 1944, Dewey again sought the Republican nomination for president. At the 1944 Republican Convention, Dewey's two main rivals were Ohio governor John Bricker and former Minnesota governor Harold Stassen. After some backroom dealing, both men withdrew from the nomination, and Dewey was selected unanimously as the Republican candidate. Dewey immediately named Bricker as his running mate.

Using his usual tactics during his campaign against Roosevelt, Dewey, without any proof, insisted there was corruption and communist influences in Roosevelt's New Deal Administration. Then Dewey was ready to throw a bombshell that would devastate America: he was going to claim that President Roosevelt had known, in advance, about the Japanese bombing of Pearl Harbor. It was only through the intervention of Army General George C. Marshall that Dewey decided against using this dirty and disprovable tactic. Roosevelt won the election handily by a 54 percent to 46 percent margin. But Dewey's showing was better than any other Republican had done running against FDR for president in four tries.

President Roosevelt died on April 12, 1945, a mere 82 days into his fourth term as president. This made Roosevelt's Vice President Harry Truman the new President of the United States. However Truman, a conservative-leaning Democrat, was a polarizing figure as president, even in his own party.

In early 1948, Truman's approval rating as president was a paltry 36%. As a result, the Democratic Party was seriously divided at its Convention in 1948. Although Harry Truman was nominated as his Party's candidate for president, two Democratic leaders, Henry A. Wallace and Strom Thurmond, broke ranks and ran for the presidency as third-party candidates. Meanwhile, Dewey easily garnered the Republican Party nomination. Because of the split among Democrats, the general feeling was Dewey only had to play it safe to win the election.

The 1948 Presidential Election ran long into the night and through the early morning hours of the next day. The liberal press was so confident of a Dewey win, on the morning of November 3, 1948, the *Chicago Tribune* ran the front page headline: "Dewey Defeats Truman!"

However, the man who railroaded Lucky Luciano into a long jail term could not convince the American public he was the right man to be the President of the United States. Even with the Democratic nomination split three ways and the liberal press in the tank for Dewey, Truman beat Dewey fairly easy. Truman garnered 303 electoral votes, while the liberal Republican Dewey received 189, Thurmond, 39, and Henry Wallace received no electoral votes at all.

Dewey declined to run for president in 1952. However, Dewey was instrumental in getting the moderate, General Dwight D. Eisenhower, the presidential nomination over Dewey's conservative foe Robert Taft.

Eisenhower won two terms as president. But in 1964, when Taft's protégó Barry Goldwater was nominated for president, Dewey, stewing in his own juices, declined to even attend the GOP Convention in San Francisco.

It was the first Republican Convention Dewey had missed since 1936.

When Dewey's third term as governor expired in 1955, Dewey decided he had gone as far as he could go in the political arena, and he could make his fortune in private law practice with his law firm Dewey Ballantine. And that Dewey did, making him a millionaire many times over by 1960.

Dewey's wife, Frances, died of cancer in 1970, and within months Dewey was dating sultry actress Kitty Carlisle. There were rumors of an imminent engagement. But before there was any formal announcement, Thomas E. Dewey died of a sudden heart attack on March 16, 1971, eight days before his 69th birthday.

Somewhere, Lucky Luciano must have been smiling. Lucky might even have met his old foe, face-to-face; most likely in a hot joint with no air conditioning.

Bonus Feature:

WHITEY BULGER - THE BIGGEST RAT

By - Joe Bruno

Editor – Lawrence Venturato

Published by:
Knickerbocker Publishing Company

*****

"RATS ARE NOT MADE; PEOPLE ARE BORN RATS."
- Mathew J. Mari, New York City Criminal Attorney for 36 years

Chapter One – "You know who I am. I'm Whitey Bulger."

The first time aspiring musician Joshua Bond met "America's
Most Wanted Fugitive," Whitey Bulger, Bond knew the spry 77-
year-old retiree as plain old Charlie Gasko.

In 2007, the 26-year-old Bond had just moved to Santa
Monica, California with plans of getting involved in the in the
Hollywood film business or music business, whichever came first.
Bond played guitar in a band called the Kings. Since work was hard
to come by, Bond needed a way to pay the rent and keep food on the
table while he pursued his dreams. As a result, Bond took a job as
co-manager of the Princess Eugenia Apartments where he received
free living quarters in apartment 304, as one of the perks that came
with the job. His next-door neighbor, living in apartment 303, was
Charlie Gasko and his wife Carol (real name Catherine Greig).

Bond liked to play the guitar in his apartment, sometimes
loud enough to be heard clearly through the walls into apartment
303. One day, after playing a particularly stirring riff, Bond heard a
knock on his apartment door. This was the first time this
phenomenon had occurred, and Bond figured he was about to get a
neighborly complaint about the noise. When Bond opened the door,
he came face to face with the man he knew as "Charlie" from next
door. Bond recoiled, waiting to receive a string of obscenities.

Instead, he received a gift.

While Bond stood there quivering, Whitey told Bond he was
fond of his music, which was a cross between country western and
the blues. That said, Whitey handed Bond a black wool Stetson hat,
sporting a leather band sprinkled with silver buttons.

"I don't wear this hat anymore," Whitey told Bond. "I think
maybe you could use it."

Bond, tickled pink at the lack of a reprimand, eagerly
accepted the hat, and then he bid Whitey goodbye.

But it was not goodbye for long.

Whitey developed the habit of knocking on Bond's door at
least twice a week, supposedly to make small talk. The truth is,
Bulger, on the run for more than a decade, didn't trust anybody, and
he wanted to know all he could about everything connected to the

Princess Eugenia Apartments. To Whitey, being pals with the co-manager was simply good business sense.

Whitey, being Whitey, found it difficult not to intrude on his young friend without bearing gifts, whether Bond needed them or not. On one visit, Whitey gave Bond a beard trimmer; a subtle hint maybe Bond was looking a little too scruffy, and Whitey didn't like scruffy.

Whitey was a fitness buff, and he thought Bond was a little out of shape for a man fifty years his junior. So, Whitey dipped into his retirement savings and bought Bond a weight set, complete with a bench and a stomach-crunching thingamajig.

Over the years, Whitey was diligent about taking good care of the assistant manager of the Princess Eugenia Apartments. During the Christmas holidays, instead of cash, one year Whitey bequeathed Bond a spiffy decorative plate. Another year Whitey gave Bond an Elvis Presley coffee table (no musician should ever be without one).

However, Whitey was a bit gruff. He insisted on proper decorum when it came to Bond recognizing his benevolence. One holiday season, Whitey left a bag full of Christmas presents at Bond's door. Later, when Whitey and Bonds crossed paths in the underground garage, Bond nary mentioned a word about the gifts. This pissed off Whitey, leading him to reprimand Bond for his lack of respect, even going as far as to "suggest" Bond jot him and Carol a sincere thank-you note. Bond duly complied, kissing off the incident off as nothing more than an old man asking for his due.

During the period from 2007 to 2011, Bond and Whitey maintained a friendly relationship. An uncle/nephew type of rapport developed between the two, where Whitey dispensed advice and Bond made believe he took it. Whitey seemed like a nice elderly man, but Bond was only interested in his music career. Putting up with Whitey was part of the job of being co-manager of the Princess Eugenia Apartments. Bond humored Whitey, and Whitey ate up what seemed to be the young man's deference to Whitey's superior intellect and lifelong experiences.

Bond knew of only one instance where old Charlie Gasko indicated he was capable of violence, and this was because Whitey told Bond about the incident himself.

The Ocean View Manor, a state-licensed residential facility for the mentally disabled, was located a few doors down from

Princess Eugenia Apartments. Mentally ill people sometimes do strange things. One resident in particular got his jollies by hiding in the bushes near the facility, and then springing out at an unsuspecting passerby to scare him out of his skin.

One night, as was his wont, Whitey took his moll, Catherine Greig, on a late-night fitness stroll. Suddenly, the eccentric from the Ocean View Manor bounded from the bushes, intending to scare Whitey and Greig.

But Whitey doesn't scare easily.

Whitey told Bond that when the lunatic rushed at him and his wife, Whitey, who always kept a big knife strapped to his ankle, grabbed the man by the neck, pulled out his knife, waved it in the man's face, and said, "If you ever do that to me again, I will cut you to pieces."

Fast-forward to June 22, 2011.

Bond had plans to go to a concert in Hollywood that evening with his pal, Neal Marsh, to see the band, My Morning Jacket. The other co-manager of the Princess Eugenia Apartments, Birgitta Farinelli, had gone on vacation. So, Bond told his assistant, Thea, to substitute for him at the manager's desk, located in the hotel across the street from Princess Eugenia Apartments, while Bond sawed a few afternoon Z's on his apartment couch.

At about 3:30 p.m., Bond's phone rang, rousing him from a deep sleep. Thea was on the line and told him F.B.I. agents were in his office. The feds said they needed to speak to Bond immediately about one of the tenants.

This unwelcome intrusion into his afternoon nap did not please Bond. He planned to motor off to Hollywood in a few hours and didn't appreciate any unnecessary distractions.

Thea handed the phone to F.B.I. agent, Scott Garriola, who told Bond that it was imperative that he come to the office immediately, if not sooner.

"Can't this wait until tomorrow?" Bond asked.

"No, it can't," Garriola said. "I need you here now!"

Knowing you don't argue with the feds, Bond dragged himself off his couch, splashed a little water on his face, and then he exited his apartment. When he reached the manager's office, Bond met Garriola and another federal agent. The agents showed Bond a string of photos of the couple Bond knew as Charlie and Carol

Gasko. The feds asked Bond if he could confirm their identities and he did so.

"Yes, I know them," Bond told Garriola. "That's Charlie and Carol from apartment 303."

"Are you absolutely sure?" Garriola asked.

"Definitely; that's them," Bond said.

Garriola told Bond who his neighbors really were, including the information that Whitey was alleged to be a serial murderer. Garriola wanted to arrest Whitey outside his apartment because Whitey's M.O. indicated he kept an arsenal of guns nearby at all times. To facilitate the arrest, Garriola asked Bond if he would be so kind as to go up to apartment 303 and knock on the door.

Bond was not brave. He also was not stupid. Bond didn't mind knocking on apartment 303's door to talk to old Charlie. But confronting a lunatic like Whitey Bulger was not high on Bond's list of things to do.

So, Garriola came up with a plan that would not put Bond in any danger.

Garriola ran down to Whitey's storage locker, located in the garage of the Princess Eugenia Apartments. Using a pair of bolt cutters, Garriola chopped Whitey's lock to pieces, giving the impression petty thieves had stolen Whitey's possessions.

After rushing back to the manager's office, Garriola ordered Bond to phone apartment 303 and tell Whitey his locker had been broken into. By this time, Bond had done a little Googling of Whitey on the office computer. What he saw did not calm his nerves.

Bond later told CBS News, "I went to his (Whitey's) Wikipedia page, and I'm kinda, like, scrolling through, and it's like, murder and extortion, and all this stuff."

Nonetheless, Bond summoned up the courage and phoned apartment 303.

No answer.

Then he tried the cellphone number Carol (Catherine Greig) had given him as a backup.

Still no answer.

Garriola checked with a fellow agent, who confirmed that surveillance definitely showed a man and a woman were present in apartment 303. Garriola tried again to convince Bond to knock on the door of apartment 303.

Bond again refused and who could blame him? He wasn't being paid by the Princess Eugenia Apartments to put his life on the line.

Before Garriola could decide what to do, the phone rang in the manager's office. It was Catherine Greig inquiring if Bond had just called her cell phone. Bond admitted he had, and then told Greig Garriola's malarkey about their storage locker having been broken into.

Grieg hesitated, and then after conferring with Whitey, she said her husband would meet Bond in the garage.

In the underground garage, Whitey didn't get close to his locker. Before he knew what was happening, more than 40 F.B.I. agents in full riot gear, with their guns and rifles pointed his way, surrounded Whitey.

Garriola barked at Whitey, "Get down on your knees!"

Whitey was dressed in white clothes with a white summer hat on his head. (Whitey was a noted Howard Hughes-type neat freak, fearful of the slightest grime.)

"Fuck you!" Whitey said. "There's oil on the floor!"

Garriola told Whitey to move a few steps to his right, and then get down on his knees.

Whitey cursed some more.

Finally, Whitey found a clean spot and got down on his knees, where the agents cuffed Whitey's hands behind his back.

"Please identify yourself," Garriola said.

"I'm Charlie Gasko," Whitey replied.

"You're not Charlie Gasko," Garriola said. "How about we go upstairs and ask your girlfriend to identify you as Charlie Gasko? She's in enough trouble already."

Whitey grunted.

"Okay. You know who I am," Whitey said. "I'm Whitey Bulger."

The 16-year manhunt for the "Most Wanted" criminal in America had finally ended.

If you'd like to read the rest of "Whitey Bulger - The Biggest Rat" go to:

I hope you enjoyed reading this book as much as I enjoyed writing it. If you want to be added to my email list, email me at jbruno999@aol.com.

If you liked *Famous Murders, Riots, Disasters, and Crooked Politicians: New York City - 1834 to 1938*, I'd appreciate it if you wrote a short review on Amazon.com at: http://www.amazon.com/dp/B00N432WSS

Just click the button that says "Create Your Own Review," and fire away!

All reviews, positive and negative, will be greatly appreciated. Sometimes I learn more from the negative reviews than I do from the positive reviews, so don't be bashful.

Joe Bruno's "Mobsters, Gangs, Crooks, and Other Creeps" was the runner up in the 2013 eFestival of Words Best of the Independent Book Awards in the category "General Nonfiction."

http://www.efestivalofwords.com/2013-efestival-of-words-winners-t473.html

About Joe Bruno:

A Vietnam veteran in the United States Navy, Joe Bruno started out in the newspaper business in the mid-1970s as a sports columnist for the New York Tribune. Bruno's sports articles have also appeared in the Middletown Record, Penthouse Magazine, Razor Magazine, Boxing Today, Boxing World, International Boxing, Referee Magazine, Inside Boxing, the Cyberboxingzone and Travelgolf.com.

In 1997-98, Bruno was the host of a weekday drive-time sports-talk radio show in Sarasota, Florida on WQSA 1220 called "In the Know with Joltin' Joe."

In 2000, Bruno's first novel *Angel of Death* was published by iUniverse.com. Bruno's second novel *Find Big Fat Fanny Fast* was published in 2010. *Snakeheads: Chinese Illegal Immigrant Smugglers - A Screenplay* was published in 2013.

Bruno's true book crime book *Mobsters, Gangs, Crooks, and Other Creeps - Volume 1 - New York City* was published in June 2011. Other books in this series include, *Mobsters, Gangs, Crooks, and Other Creeps - Volume 2 - New York City* (December 2011), *Mobsters, Gangs, Crooks, and Other Creeps - Volume 3 - New York City* (March 2012), *Mobsters, Gangs, Crooks and Other Creeps - Volume 4* (December 2012), and *Mobsters, Gangs, Crooks and Other Creeps-Volume 5 - Girlfriends and Wives (April 2013).*

Other true crime books by Joe Bruno include:
Murder and Mayhem in the Big Apple - From the Black Hand to Murder Incorporated March 2012),

The Wrong Man: Who Ordered the Murder of Gambler Herman Rosenthal & Why (May 2012),
Mob Wives - Fuhgeddaboudit! (August 2012) and
Whitey Bulger - The Biggest Rat (September 2013).

Joe Bruno's most recent book is *Mob Rats - Gangsters Who Squeal* (May 2014)

Boxed sets written by Joe Bruno include:"
Joe Bruno's Mobsters - Two Volume Set (December 2013)
Joe Bruno's Mobsters - Three Volume Set (March 2013),
Joe Bruno's Mobsters - Five Volume Set (April 2013),
Joe Bruno's Mobsters - Six Volume Set (September 2012), and
Joe Bruno's Mobsters - Eight Volume Set (April 2013).

Visit Joe Bruno's Amazon Author Page at:
http://www.amazon.com/Joe-Bruno/e/B0047OPD9S/ref=ntt_athr_dp_pel_pop_1

Website: josephbrunowriter.com, or at mobstersgangs.com.
Blog: http://joebrunoonthemob.wordpress.com/.
Facebook page: *Mobsters, Gangs* is at:
https://www.facebook.com/mobstersgangs.

What people are saying about Joe Bruno's Books:

5.0 out of 5 stars

Fabulous!!!!!

By **Brenda**
Verified Purchase

I really enjoyed Joe Bruno's *Mobsters, Gangs, Crooks, and Other Creeps, Volumes 1-5*. Joe Bruno's books are easy to get into with the short chapters and out there approach. I love his sarcastic banter and his in depth knowledge of these bad guys. The books are wildly compelling especially since is the real deal. No fictional made up story here. I love that!

These books are thoroughly entertaining, mind blowing and irresistible. If you are interested in mob stories about famous and not so famous crooks, you will love this book and the others that Joe Bruno has written. These books are easy to get into and you can just pick it up and read a chapter at a time. They are a captivating entertain read, to say the least!

5.0 out of 5 stars

A lesson about "The Other" Mob.

By **Rony Barbery**
Verified Purchase

I found all Joe Bruno's books refreshing as a departure from the great books Mr. Bruno has written about what is considered the traditional "Mafia". As always, Joe Bruno has demonstrated that no matter how much or how carefully you read the news, you never know the whole story until he puts it in writing. The book is full of small details that you never heard about, but are huge in painting a portrait of the real mobsters in this world. If you don't already have one of Joe Bruno's books, get on the ball and get a copy!

5.0 out of 5 stars

Another great one!

By **lcook0825**

As I have said in the past Mr. Bruno is the best writer of books concerning the Mafia that I have read, and I read everything I can. This was a great read from beginning to end. It was accurate according to everything else I have read regarding the Mafia. Thanks again for a great book, Joe, and keep me posted on your next release.

5.0 out of 5 stars

Fascinating!

By **koalaman35**

Joe Bruno's books are a wonderful trip through the history of mobsters, thugs, and other ne'er-do-wells in the mob. I love Joe's writing style.

Bibliography

The research I did for *Famous Murders, Riots, Disasters, and Crooked Politicians - New York City - 1834 to 1938* came from the more than 75 crime/history books that I personally own (some I stole from the library, but don't tell the library police). Almost all of these books were purchased from Amazon.com. I have Amazon Prime ($99 a year), so I always receive free two-day shipping on all my purchases. This comes in handy, when I realize I need a certain book to complete a chapter, and presto, in two days, said book arrives miraculously at my front door. I also have my new Amazon Kindle, which, with its Amazon Whispernet, magically sends me a book I need for research over the Internet almost instantaneously. But all things being equal, I'd rather have the actual print book in my hands.

I guess I'm just funny that way.

I've also used several Internet websites including *Wikipedia, Six For Five, Tru TV Crime Library, Newspaperarchives.com,* and the online archives of the *New York Times.*

The books that I used for my research include the following:

Asbury, Herbert. *All Around Town.* New York: Thunder Mouth Press, 1934.

Asbury, Herbert. *The Gangs of New York.* New York: Alfred A. Knopf Inc., 1928.

Breslin, Jimmy. *Damon Runyon - A Life.* New York: Dell Publishing, 1991.

Cohen, Rich. *Tough Jews.* New York: Vintage Books, 1998.

Dash, Mike. *The First Family.* New York: Ballantine Books, 2009

Dash, Mike. *Satan's Circus*. New York: Three Rivers Press, 2007

Duke, Thomas J. *Celebrated Cases of America*. San Francisco: Board of Police Commissioners of San Francisco, 1910.

Ellis, Edward Robb. *The Epic of New York City*. New York: Kodansha America Inc., 1966.

Fried, Albert, *The Rise and Fall of the Jewish Gangster.* New York: Columbia University Press, 1980, 1993.

Gilfoyle, Timothy J. *A Pickpocket's Tale*. New York: W.W. Norton & Company, 2006.

Homer, Fredrick D. *Guns and Garlic*. West Lafayette, Indiana: Purdue University Press, 1974.

Johnson, Nelson. *Boardwalk Empire*. New Jersey. Plexus Publishing Inc., 2002

Keefe, Rose. *The Starker*. Nashville, TN: Cumberland House Publishing, 2008.

Kobler, John. *The Life and World of Al Capone*. New York: G.P. Putnam's Sons, 1971.

Kwitny, Jonathan. *Vicious Circles*. New York: W.W. Norton & Company, 1979.

Mitchell, Elizabeth, *The Fearless Mrs. Goodwin,* Kindle Edition, Byliner, 2011.

Newton, Michael. *The Encyclopedia of Gangsters*. New York: Thunder's Mouth Press, 2007.

Reis, Jacob. *How the Other Half Lives*. United States of America: Seven Treasure Publications, 2009.

Rovere, Richard H. *Howe & Hummel.* New York: Syracuse University Press, 1947, 1985.

Sante, Luc. *Low Life.* New York: Farrar Straus Giroux, 1991.

Shirley, Glenn. *Hello Sucker - The Story of Texas Guinan.* Austin, Texas: Eakin Press, 1989.

Sifakis, Carl. *The Encyclopedia of Crime.* New York: Smithmark, 1992.

Sifakis, Carl. *The Mafia Encyclopedia.* New York: Facts on File, 1987.

Sutton, Charles, *The History of the New York Tombs.* New York: A. Roman & Co., 1874.

Turkus, Burton & Feder, Sid. *Murder Inc.* Cambridge MA: Da Capo Press, 1951, 1979.